LETS
GO
PUBLISH!

How to Write Your 1st Book & Publish It Using Amazon KDP

You won't believe you can do it until you try!

When I began to write they called publishing your own book, the Vanity Press. To avoid the scourge, you had to do handstands talking to publishers who did not want to read your manuscript. Most gave up. I was lucky, I had a friend who worked for a Publisher, Harper & Rowe and I got a break that I could not get again if I tried today.

Instead of a vanity press, which implies you are writing your autobiography because you are too unimportant for a publisher to want it, today self-publishing is the preferred way to bring out a new book. Tens of thousands of great authors have had enough with snobby publishers and author's agents.

So, they either start their own companies, or they use phenomenally easy to work with organizations such as Amazon KDP to publish for them. In these cases the author has some work to do but believe me it is easy to get published. Amazon KDP will assure that you have a work, of which you can be proud.

You came to the right place by picking this book.

Not only do we walk you through Amazon Kindle Direct Processing (KDP) and how to get your completed manuscript published, we also show you how to complete your manuscript so it is acceptable to any other publisher in the world.

We show you the ins and outs of writing a book using Microsoft Word as your author tool. We show you how to structure your book, create table of contents and indexes; how to format your chapters and lots more. We then show you how to upload your document file to Amazon so that you too can one day be a famous author.

LETS GO PUBLISH

BRIAN W. KELLY

Published by: LETS GO PUBLISH!
Publisher: Brian P. Kelly
Editor: Brian P..Kelly
Mail Location: P.O. Box 621, Wilkes-Barre, PA 18703
Web site   www.letsgopublish.com

Library of Congress Copyright Information Pending
Original Book Cover Design by Brian W. Kelly

ISBN Information: The International Standard Book Number (ISBN) is a unique machine-readable identification number, which marks any book unmistakably. The ISBN is the clear standard in the book industry. 159 countries and territories are officially ISBN members. The Official ISBN For this book is on the outside cover: **978-1-951562-18-2**

| The price for this work is : | | | | | | | | | $14.95 USD |

| 10 | 9 | 8 | 7 | 6 | 5 | 4 | 3 | 2 | 1 |

Release Date: September 2016

Dedication

*I dedicate this book
To the magnificent Joseph McKeown Family*

*They are the family of Joseph and Ruth McKeown, RIO. I list
them in order of birth: angel Joseph Jr. and angel Kathleen,
Their children and spouses include Patti & Joe Niznik and
children Matthew and Joshua; Mike & Lisa, and children Katie,
Michael and Angela ; Kevin & Megan; and children Patrick
and Liam.*

*And then there are also Kellys on the Kathleen McKeown side,
Angels Cornelius and Angel Kathleen Kelly, Angel Helen and
Angel Joe Drexinger, Alice and angels Bonnie and Joseph Jr.*

*All his life, Joe McKeown (Jr.) RIP always had two wonderful
cohorts--   Melvin (Manhattan) Manhart, and Joseph "Red"
Jones, RIP.*

Thank you all and the Best!

Acknowledgments

I would like to thank many, many people for helping me in this effort.

I appreciate all the help that I have received in putting this book together as well as all of my other 232 published books.

My printed acknowledgments had become so large that book readers "complained" about going through too many pages to get to page one of the text.

And, so to permit me more flexibility, I put my acknowledgment list online, and it continues to grow. Believe it or not, it once cost about a dollar more to print each book.

Thank you and God bless you all for your help.

Please check out www.letsgopublish.com to read the latest version of my heartfelt acknowledgments updated for this book. Click the bottom of the Main menu!

To sum up my acknowledgments, as I do in every book that I have written, I am compelled to offer that I am truly convinced that "the only thing you can do alone in life is fail." Thanks to my family, good friends, and a wonderful helping team, I was not and continue to be --- not alone.

Table of Contents

Dedication v

Acknowledgments vii

Chapter 1 First Thoughts about Writing a Book.................................. 1

Chapter 2 Getting the Right Perspective... 13

Chapter 3 Structuring Your Book for Publishing 20

Chapter 4 Your Book Cover 37

Chapter 5 A look at the Parts of a Book by Example 41

Chapter 6 Final Preparations for Publishing..................................... 63

Chapter 7 Using Amazon KDP for Publishing................................. 75

Chapter 8 Getting Started with Kindle Direct Publishing KDP 77

Chapter 9 Creating Your First Book Title with Amazon KDP 83

Other Books by Brian Kelly: (amazon.com, and Kindle).................... 97

Preface:

Why did Brian W. Kelly write this book?

In a word, it was *CreateSpace,* the best author publishing tool that could be found at the time. . "My good friend Paul Harkins, an accomplished writer had been published by numerous Publishing Houses when he discovered CreateSpace. I was still using Offset Paperback's print on demand for my books and though it worked well, it was much more difficult to get work through. I have taken papers etc. that I had previously written, dressed them up and created books in several days using CreateSpace.

Plus, right after they would approve my work, and I approved their work, which by the way is impeccable, they made the book available on Amazon and Kindle. It is easier than I could ever have imagined and this book is my 232nd."

Since those early days, Amazon's Kindle Division bought out Create Space and merged the two companies into what is now called Amazon Kindle Direct Publishing (KDP). It has all the features of CreateSpace and I use it with the same relative ease.

Brian Kelly had been previously published by John Wiley and Sons, the Ballinger Publishing Division of Harper Collins, Cardinal Business Media, Midrange Computing, and 29th Street Press. Then, Kelly stopped writing for several years. Brian was always frustrated by how long it took to create a contract to publish a book.

He felt like he could write a book faster than it would take to negotiate its publishing. After his several year hiatus, and the untimely death of his author's agent, Kelly was left trying to figure out how to get his next book, which was already conceived and partly written out to the marketplace.

Author's agents do not want to take a gamble on anybody nowadays unless they are TV stars or already successful novelists. It is a sin. Great writers are being left without a means to express themselves other than the informal blogosphere.

Worse than that perhaps is that publishers no longer will respond to an uninvited query about a manuscript. They want to be left alone with their author's agents. It is very frustrating for somebody who has a lot to say and their favored means of expression, the book, is no longer available.

What Brian Kelly did was start his own Imprint called Lets Go Publish! He was writing technical books when he formed the small company. His former tech publishers agreed to distribute his books and this was fine for a number of years before they decided that they wanted to work only with their own authors.

Kelly founded BookHawkers Internet Book Publisher so that he could sell the books published by Lets Go Publish! Kelly also changed his preference from tech books to patriotic and political books, human interest and sports. Kelly sold all these books on BookHawkers and had them printed at Offset Paperback, a division of Bertlesmann Printing Group.

They are a very good company but, according to Brian, they have none of the magical ingredients of CreateSpace. When Brian found CreateSpace and engaged them, he immediately became well-known again and his books began to sell faster than ever before—across the globe.

Anybody seeking out this book knows that the publishing industry is evolving. Hundreds of thousands of authors like you have begun to publish profitable work instead of waiting for agents and publishers to give the green light. Quite frankly, long before the green light, the publishing tag team often choose not to return phone calls.

With Amazon's KDP, you can easily access tools, quality printing, booksellers, eBook distribution, and marketing strategies so that you can generate more opportunities than you imagined – all while building your following of readers. Brian Kelly knows this is true after just four years of active publishing.

Brian wanted to repeat in this preface what we have written on the first page of this book:

When I began to write they called publishing your own book, the Vanity Press. To avoid the scourge, you had to do handstands talking to publishers who did not want to read your manuscript. Most gave up. I was lucky, I had a friend who worked for a Publisher, Harper & Rowe and I got a break that I could not get again if I tried today.

Instead of a vanity press, which implies you are writing your autobiography because you are too unimportant for a publisher to want it, today self-publishing is the preferred way to bring out a new book. Tens of thousands of great authors have had enough with snobby publishers and author's agents.

So, they either start their own companies, or they use phenomenally easy to work with organizations such as Amazon KDP to publish for them. In these cases the author has some work to do but believe me it is easy to get published. CreateSpace will assure that you have a work, of which you can be proud.

You came to the right place by picking this book.

Not only do we walk you through Amazon Kindle Direct Processing (KDP) and how to get your completed manuscript published, we also show you how to complete your manuscript so it is acceptable to any other publisher in the world.

We show you the ins and outs of writing a book using Microsoft Word as your author tool. We show you how to structure your book, create table of contents and indexes; how to format your chapters and lots more. We then show you how to upload your document file to Amazon so that you too can one day be a famous author.

You are going to love this book as it is a good read. If you want an express route to getting your first book published with no guilt, this book is for you.

I wish you all the best

Brian P. Kelly, Publisher
P.O Box 621 Wilkes-Barre, Pennsylvania 18703

About the Author

Brian W. Kelly is a retired Assistant Professor from the Business Information Technology (BIT) program at Marywood University, where he also served as the IBM i and Midrange Systems Technical Advisor to the IT faculty. Kelly developed and taught many college and professional courses in the IT and business areas. He is also a contributing technical editor to IT Jungle's "The Four Hundred" and "Four Hundred Guru" Newsletters.

A former IBM Senior Systems Engineer, he has an active consultancy in the information technology field, (www.kellyconsulting.com). He is the author of hundreds of books and numerous articles about current IT topics. Kelly is a frequent speaker at COMMON, IBM conferences, and other technical conferences and user group meetings across the United States.

This is Brian Kelly's 232nd book.

Chapter 1 First Thoughts about Writing a Book

Early Suggestions

Since you are a prospective writer thinking about publishing a book, let me make a suggestion. You first need to write a book. I am not kidding. Leave all your publishing thoughts on the table and move from the table to your writing desk with your PC ready to slam out a few great paragraphs followed by even better paragraphs. Eventually, you will have chapters and ultimately, you will have a book.

My suggestion is that the book should be as close to 150 pages as possible—no less and not much more. It should be set for about a 6 X 9" book-size in a 12-point Calisto MT font.

Do not worry about publishing the book until you have your masterpiece written and edited at least three times. I will show you how to publish your book three different ways. It is lots easier to publish the book than to write a masterpiece. You will be able to get your book published one way or another. Writing the killer book is much more important than getting it published. One will follow the other if you are persistent and tenacious.

Add pictures / graphics as you write

Many authors choose to include their own artwork, illustrations, or photographs on their covers or interiors. Many take images freely available on the Internet and use them to highlight an idea. This is a great way to make your book more appealing to readers. Adding pictures to your word document manuscript is as easy as cutting and pasting from your source or using the insert image capabilities of Word to bring an image from a file on your PC.

Though there are very specific requirements an image must meet in order to be published, CreateSpace and other publishing houses are often forgiving. If perhaps you think that the resolution is fine and the picture is good enough, most publishers will permit it to be in the book even if the image is not as crisp as it can be. We cannot teach you all about images in this book but we will say that you should use them to the extent they amplify the text and make it interesting. Don't worry about the technicalities.

Now, let's talk about where we can put images in any book.

Images for the Front Cover

Michele Thomas or some graphic artist should design your cover for you. You will provide somebody such as Michele any specific pictures you would like to use. The graphic artist will always try to find the clearest version of the images you provide and they'll offer advice if they cannot get better quality images. There are many sources of images from the Internet per se to Internet sites, as well as fee and free image houses such as those at http://www.thinkstockphotos.com, Hemera or iStockphoto. The latter groups charge for images.

I eventually began to use the cover creator on CreateSpace and now I use it on KDP (Kindle Direct Publishing)—Amazon's new hard cover book printing company. Amazon bought CreateSpace a few years ago and recently converted all my older books to KDP acceptable publications. My books (currently 231) are almost all available from amazon.com/author/brianwkelly.

Images for Your Interior

The instructions in this book are for authors who have chosen to create a black/white interior book with a color cover. If you are publishing a color book, the instructions in this book still apply but there are more things that you make be able to do to enhance your book.

Color and B/W images include photographs, drawings, artwork, screen shots, charts, or any other graphic that would need to be inserted into your manuscript. If you are selecting stock images for your interior, there is typically a fee for each image you choose. If after you reread your book, you find that it could use more images of various kinds, feel free to add them in Chapters that need what they can provide.

Figure 3-5 Walking Across the George Washington Bridge

If you are writing a book in which you are not referring to images or charts in sections of the text, then it is up to you whether you label your images or not. Authors label their images at the top or bottom with no spacing. A common nomenclature for images is to use the word *Figure* followed by the Chapter number followed by the sequence of the image in the chapter. The fifth image in chapter 3 would this be labeled Figure 3-5. This label can be followed by something descriptive such as The George Washington Bridge as shown on the prior page.

Permission to Use

Just as you make sure that the text you are quoting is not extensive so that a fair use issue would not occur, you must make sure your images are legal. Publishers often insist that you have permission from the image owner. However, generally available internet pictures in the public domain and those you buy from a picture stock are fine.

Image Size & Resolution: What You Need to Know

Though they say that an image is only as good as its resolution, relative to its size, size and resolution together determine the quality of your image and how it will look in your final book. Problems with image size or resolution are the number one reason may be reason for production delays but in my experience with print on demand printers as well as CreateSpace, if you approve the look of the image in your proof, for the most part, they will print it as is. Here are some good facts for you to understand about images in general.

Image Resolution

You can think of resolution as the crispness or quality of focus in your image. Obviously, we want the best possible resolution. Resolution is measured in PPI, or pixels per inch. You may also see it measured in DPI, or dots per inch. They both mean roughly the same thing and can be used interchangeably. Images for your book should be no less than 300 PPI or DPI. Anything less will not print with accurate clarity and may appear fuzzy or jagged in your final book. Though this is 100% accurate often, an image with less resolution can still do the trick.

Image Size

An image's resolution is directly related to its size. For interior text files, place your images at the size you want them to be by inserting them specifically within the text of the Chapters where they best fit.

How I started writing

Many writers will tell you that the best way to start writing a book is to start writing something soon. There is a lot of truth there. Your first book will be much more difficult than any other book you may choose to write. Everything you do will be new. Regardless, the most important thing is to start writing.

When I wrote this book originally several years ago, it was my 83rd separate and identifiable book. I also put out a few radically different second editions. Now, my last book, written on April 28, 2020 is my 231st and I have already begun my 232nd titled *Great Moments in LSU Football.*

In my writing life, I have also written essays—both technical and theme oriented. Several of my books came from writing an essay that continued into Part I, Part II, Part III, etc. Essays do not ready very well when there are a lot of parts but, all other things being equal, books with a few chapters and a reasonable number of pages are easy to pull off and complete and perhaps more importantly, they are more enjoyable to read. Of course, the content in all cases matters.

I wrote my first book well over thirty years ago. I did not have my own advice to go by back then so I did not listen to it. After I had written about a quarter of a book, or so I thought. my friend Dennis took me to a real English taskmaster, Myrna Schaeffer, RIP, who really helped me and encouraged me. After you write a bit, hopefully somebody you know can find you a Myrna Schaeffer. She made me feel like a schoolkid who should have already known the points she put forth but the lessons were well worth it. I should have taped them

When I began to write, I had a brand spanking new 1981 IBM PC with diskette drives and I used EasyWriter as my word processor. I had no idea about page sizes so I used the whole page 8.5" X 11." That's fine for writing bulk text. Myrna had to read printed pages and so it helped to have a lot on a page as back then it cost less to print. She did not edit the whole thing but gave me enough of a perspective to know what I needed to do to keep going.

BTW, I have been told that Amazon printing today set the price of a book for printing (your cost when you sell a book through them) using just the # of pages. I have a few books that I re-released from 6"X9" to 8.5 X 11 and it was able to reduce the price by several dollars with the same content.

I did keep going. Chapter after chapter, I wrote as if each chapter was its own essay remotely connected to the theme of the book. The book was a technical history book. Eventually, I had about 400 or more pages single sided. It was in a huge a huge binder. Back then, I wrote each chapter as a new document, figuring I would combine them in the end. This would work today also but today; I write one book with multiple chapters.

I had the good fortune of having Carolyn Langan, another English teacher, in my new neighborhood after moving from my first home in 1987. She is still a princess in terms of a person to work with. Since I had never written a book, it was all new. I had no idea what she would find.

Carolyn had the manuscript in printed form for about a month as I recall. One day she brought it over. She had gotten somewhat past the first 100 pages. I forget which chapter. She said the book was very technical for her to know in many cases whether something was right or wrong grammatically. She made lots of changes but believed it would take her forever to edit the whole thing. Plus, she knew that after I made the changes, I would need her again as I put additional touches on the book. She had a full-time job and she simply could not get this done in any appropriate time frame.

I took all of her work and I made all of the individual changes to the files, which by this time I had moved to WordPerfect, another word processing software package. WordPerfect made editing text on the machine much easier than EasyWriter.

When I finished making all of Carolyn's changes and I rewrote things per her suggestions, I decided to read the book to that point. As I read the book, I hoped that nobody would ever make me read such a book again. It was terrible. It was too big and I had not sectioned it off well and had not made decisions about which ideas needed to be presented in which sequence.

The essay idea did not pull the book together well for me as the essays did not follow each other well. I decided that I was a lousy writer and I put the book down for about thirty years until the summer of 2015. I finished it early in 2016.

My first published book was titled, The Personal Computer Buyers Guide. I was fortunate to have a good friend Al Teufel who was the IBM Representative to Harper & Rowe, Publishers. Al set it up so that my writing partner for this book, Dennis Grimes and I would meet with Mike Connolly, the President of Ballinger Publishing in Cambridge, Massachusetts in the heart of the Harvard / MIT world. Mike liked our idea for the book and so we were off with book one without one page written. That's how it can be done when you have an "in.".

Mike later left Ballinger and became an author's agent and he took Dennis and I on as Clients. We had another idea. We designed some programs to collect PC specifications for six different PCs and or software packages, and Mike sold the package to John Wiley & Sons. It took us six months to produce six huge Buyers Guides for Wiley. We made some money on the books but not the level Mike Connolly had hoped. His idea was that every book an author writes should render $50,000 in additional lifetime earnings.

After the Buyers' Guides, we both stopped writing for years. Dennis never was interested enough to come back and write as a team. About 1995, I got some ideas for other technical books. My first effort was titled, The AS/400; The Internet; and Email. It sold really well. Midrange Computing dedicated a Myrna Schaeffer-type editor to get it finished, it was one tech book after another until about 2004 when I decided to write Patriotic / Political Books. My first effort was titled Taxation Without Representation. That is now in its fourth edition.

As I noted earlier, I picked up my first writing attempt again in summer 2015. I had become a much better writer by "writing." The first thing I did was analyze it. It still did not have a title. I used the Word Table of Contents generator after converting it to Microsoft Word so I could look at the many chapters in one line format. From the old chapter list, I produced an outline for how I would attack this very, very large book, which was about to grow larger.

I finished the book in the winter of 2016. A great friend of mine, Paul Harkins, who is also an author of technical computer books loved the book. I had released it with the title: Thank You, IBM: The Story of how IBM helped today's technology millionaires and billionaires gain their vast fortunes.

Paul read the book and for his consulting practice, he bought a bunch more. He sent me a note one day that I had left out a number of billionaires and he began to list them. He was right. I had not included a section on Application Software Billionaires such as SAP/AG and other ERP and Enterprise software vendors.

I stopped my projects that were in process and I wrote a new section and a bunch of new chapters, and I rearranged the book to accommodate the new billionaires in the proper section. I announced the book as a Second Edition as it had substantial changes, I also had to raise the price because nothing from the First Edition was deleted. By the way, the publisher's name for most of my books is Lets Go Publish! (LGP), a company which I began about twenty years ago. My newer books are all available here: https://www.amazon.com/author/brianwkelly

The next page shows my most extensive glance at a table of contents for any of my 83 books so far. Check out the # of chapters:

Table of Contents

Section I   Introduction
Chapter 1 Many Opportunities, Many Disappointments
Chapter 2 Fast Forward to Today. Has IBM improved?
Chapter 3 IBM Once Thought It Could Say No & Survive
Chapter 4 The IBM Story Continues
Chapter 5. IBM Was Destined for Fortune

Section II   The Watson Years
Chapter 6. IBM's Thomas Watson Sr.: Continuous Excellence
Chapter 7. Early IBM Line of Electromechanical Devices
Chapter 8. IBM's Early Efforts with Real Computers
Chapter 9. Thomas Watson Jr. IBM Presidency and Chair
Chapter 10. The Mainframe Era Begins!
Chapter 11. Modern Mainframes
Chapter 12. IBM Small Business Computers
Chapter 13. IBM System/3 Starts a New Age

Chapter 14. IBM System/38—Most Advanced System Ever
Chapter 15. AS/400 Comes Invited to the System/38 Party
Chapter 16. IBM Merges Systems i & p (AS/400 & RS/6000)
Chapter 17. Thomas Watson Jr. Steps Down as Chair & CEO

Section III   T. V. Learson & Frank T. Cary--IBM past Watsons
Chapter 18. Starting with Learson
Chapter 19. Frank Cary, the Mainframe, Mini, and Micro CEO
Chapter 20. DEC Invents the Minicomputer
Chapter 21. Hewlett-Packard Enters Minicomputer Arena
Chapter 22. Data General Formed as Minicomputer Company
Chapter 23. EMC Buys DG; Enters Minicomputer Market
Chapter 24. IBM's Non-Minicomputer Minicomputers
Chapter 25. IBM's new Series/1-- Bona Fide Minicomputer
Chapter 26. MIT, IBM and the Early Development of Unix
Chapter 27. What is Unix and Why Does It Matter?
Chapter 28. Among Many Unixes, Another Unix—Linux
Chapter 29. The Microcomputer Revolution
Chapter 30. TI—a Micro Tech Pioneer and Eternal Innovator
Chapter 31. Shockley & Fairchild Semiconductor Pioneers
Chapter 32. Motorola the Chip Maker with Different Roots
Chapter 33. The Founding of Intel
Chapter 34. Zilog: Great Microcomputer Pioneer
Chapter 35. MOS Technologies / Commodore
Chapter 36. Radio Shack: 1st Personal Computer Company
Chapter 37. Apple Piqued the Home Computerist in Us All
Chapter 38. Key IBM Software Invention: Relational Database
Chapter 39. Oracle Announces First Relational DB Product
Chapter 40. IBM Data Comm. Why Big Blue Failed?
Chapter 41. Teleprocessing: Next Step after Cards & Printers
Chapter 42. IBM and Local Area Networks
Chapter 43. Cisco Beats IBM in Networking

Section IV   CEOs John Opel & John Akers Almost Sunk IBM
Chapter 44. John Opel—CEO with Spirit, Opportunity, Failure
Chapter 45. A Deeper Look at John Akers' Years
Chapter 46. IBM Invented RISC Technology in 1974
Chapter 47. Sun Microsystems Makes It Big With RISC
Chapter 48. IBM RS/6000–A Great RISC/UNIX System
Chapter 49. Power Architecture World's Fastest Supercomputers
Chapter 50. IBM PC Introduced in Opel Years
Chapter 50   Appendix. The PC Story IBM at its Worst
Chapter 51. Compaq Beats IBM BIOS; Becomes Top PC Co
Chapter 52. Gateway Computer Company – 2000
Chapter 53. Dell Computer still on top
Chapter 54. IBM Says Good-By to the PC Industry
Chapter 55. Microsoft-- Champion of PC / x86 Software

Section V   Application Software: From Watson to Rometty
Chapter 56. What is Application Software?
Chapter 57. Business Application S'ware, Service Bureaus, Clouds
Chapter 58. IBM Once Was the Application Software Leader
Chapter 59. Impact Catamore Lawsuit-- IBM App Software
Chapter 60. IBM's Post S/3 -- Formal App Software Packages

Chapter 61. IBM Failed in the Application Software Industry
Chapter 62. Shared Medical Systems
Chapter 63. Quick Look at IBM's MAPICS Application & SAP
Chapter 64. SAP: The Best In ERP Software
Chapter 65. Small Companies – App. Software Millionaires
Chapter 66. Large Software Firms-Many Rich Entrepreneurs

Section VI Gerstner, Palmisano, & Rometty,IBM's Latest CEOs
Chapter 67 Lou Gerstner: First CEO Not Bred in IBM's culture
Chapter 68 The END: IBM's S.Palmisano and Ginni Rometty
Advertising   Lets Go Publish Publishers Other Books

How to start writing

To repeat for emphasis, many writers will tell you that the best way to start writing a book is to start writing something. The key is to stop procrastinating; make sure you understand your word processor; and get something written. Always remember that your first book will be much more difficult than any other book you may choose to write. But, you have a lifetime to write each and every book that you plan. Everything you do will be new so you will second guess a lot of things. By getting into it as quickly as you can, instead of suffering from analysis paralysis, you will be that far ahead. To say again, the most important thing is to start writing.

Nobody writes a book without an outline. Depending on who you may be, however, the outline can be completely in your head. It's been a long time since I created an outline.

Sometimes when I know there are about say, ten things that I want to accomplish in a book, instead of an outline, I write up the Chapter Headings within the book file with the same text that they will have when the book is completed. Of course, while writing the book, sometimes a cleverer chapter title may come to mind and that is fine. Just make the change and continue.

The table of contents from Thank You IBM is not one that I could have ever come up with thirty years ago. Over the thirty years it took to write the book, I became a much better writer and I became a much better text organizer. That is why my recommendation for your first book is about 100-150 pages. it permits many iterations on the way to perfection and there should be few convolutions or permutations with which to deal.

In the *Writers Dig* by Brian Klems, Brian outlines seven steps that he finds helpful in planning the completion of your book. Here they are without the detailed explanations. You may see the whole seven steps with detailed explanations in article form at http://www.writersdigest.com/online-editor/7-steps-to-creating-a-flexible-outline-for-any-story. **I checked just now and that article is still available.**

1. Craft your premise.
Your premise is the basic idea for your story.

2. Roughly sketch scene ideas.
Armed with a solid premise, you can now begin sketching your ideas for this story. Write a list of everything you already know about your story.

3. Interview your characters.
In order to craft a cast of characters that can help your plot reach its utmost potential, you'll need to discover crucial details about them, not necessarily at the beginning of their lives but at the beginning of the story. Many books such as the ones I write have no characters or the character is a machine or it is a political notion.

4. Explore your settings.
In fiction writing, your setting might be a childhood neighborhood or the seventh moon of Barsoom (Star Wars). Figure out what you might like to happen in these settings and write what you can—as much as you can.

5. Write your complete outline.
To the extent that you have it in your head and on paper from steps 1 to 4 above, go ahead and try to craft your outline.

6. Condense your outline.
Most often your first cut outline with be too big to be workable so the experts advise making the first version your extended outline and then condensing it to a more manageable form.

7. Put your outline into action.

Many writers will suggest that each time you sit down to write more in your book, begin by reviewing your outline. Read the notes for whatever you are working on at the time. Go over any problems you see in your head before "touching" the "paper" or your Word Processor. Don't hesitate to rule out prior ideas when you get a good replacement idea.

End of list—

For new writers especially, an outline will provide very valuable structure and guidance as you write your first draft. But, remember this. It is not an academic exercise. It is real. The outline does not always have to be what you originally write. You may go other places in your book.

There is no teacher such as Miss Gradenheimer scoring this assignment to assure a 100% match of outline to content. The book, not the outline is what you are writing. Do not be afraid to explore new ideas as they occur. There may be many iterations as you go from start to finish. In most cases, you will like your final product much more if you let your mind wander and write down those thoughts as part of the "story." You can always change anything in your book—even sometimes after you publish it. You can delete chapters and you can delete paragraphs to make the book be what you want it to be.

Chapter 2 Getting the Right Perspective

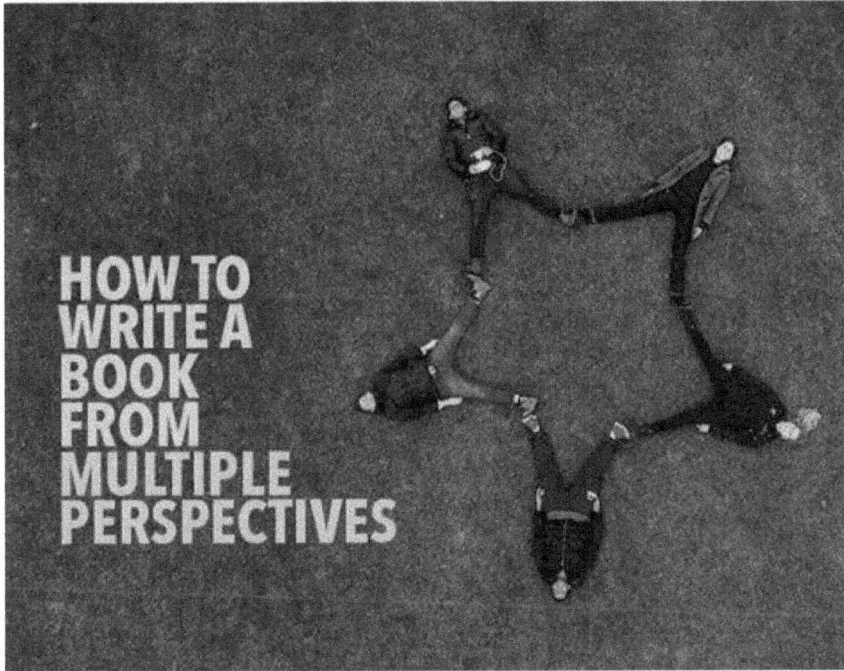

Conceiving, Writing, Editing

Several years ago even before I found CreateSpace to be the most productive avenue for me to get my Lets Go Publish! Imprinted books published, several faculty members at Marywood University and a number of students had asked what they needed to do to publish a book in a typical fashion. They meant so that the book contents would be ready to turn over to Harper Collins, Lets Go Publish! or Joe Schmoe Pubs for publishing!

Today, I picked up the results of what I had written as a teaching tool and since I have not taught at Marywood since 2011, this manuscript about writing that I am now completing is at least five years old. When I wrote the beginning of this how-to-publish guide I had just self-proofed for the second time my newest book at the time, which happened to be 562 pages. I have no idea which of my books it was but it was probably a patriotic book as I finished most tech books in the early 2000's.

As always when anyone proofs a book, there are always changes. This time was not an exception to that rule. Let me now give a bit of an explanation to the writing, editing, and proofing processes.

Regarding proofing, it helps to know that experts charge at least a dollar a page (back then) and often much more if they are good. You will be inclined to pay it if you have the funds and you are not yet a great writer and you need a great proofer. Because of the cost and the time involved in getting a book out, after paying for a few books, I decided I would begin to proof my own books. For me, it has worked out well. My secret to proofing my own book is to let it sit for a week or more so it looks like *some other goof* wrote it. You'll know why after iteration one why authors proof their work.

If hiring a proof-reader is beyond your budget, go ahead and start writing anyway as you will improve. If you have a moderate means, make sure your first book is not huge and find an English teacher as I did, to help you along. Your HS English teacher might be willing to proof for a small fee.

I would advise a neophyte to write and publish about two to five books before beginning to proof your own. For the last thirty and probably even more of my later books, I decided that I would proof them all myself.

To create a fine work, there are four requirements for initial proofing (rereading and correcting):

1. Proofing the day before's work
2. Spell checking the whole book with Word
3. Proofing a whole book in preparation for printing.
4. Final Proofing

I love writing without interruption so I like to get my thoughts down on paper really as quickly as I can type. I cannot type as quickly as I can think so my challenge is to keep my fingers from over spilling garbage on the pages while these otherwise fine appendages are trying to figure out the signals of the last buffer load of instructions from my active brain.

Eventually, the paper is full (on the screen) and the next page is full and so on and so on until, a day and night's worth of writing about a particular topic is finished. I should not say this but I will. My fingers are more coordinated and move faster while my thoughts race assisted by two or three glasses of fine red wine in the evenings.

I am literally at peak and I can solve any problem by the time the last red wine glass is served—by me. By the way, another one of my secrets is that the gallonage is stored in the garage and thus, a natural bio break and thought break is achieved on each reload.

Problems that were not solvable before the biology and reload break are most often solved by the time—about ten minutes later that I resume activity in my writer's nook with my now Windows 10 machine and Microsoft Word 2013.

I personally do not like cheap keyboards. I type faster and more accurately with a good keyboard. I think you would also. Good keyboards do not typically come with new PCs. You have to buy one with tactile and audio feedback from a company such as Unicomp, where I got mine.

I had the original IBM keyboard for years as IBM's Raleigh Plant always made the best keyboards. Before the PC, IBM sold many terminals with its finest keyboards as part of the package.

Now, I have a keyboard from Unicomp at http://www.pckeyboard.com/. Just like the old IBM keyboards, which are top quality, for about $85.00, you can buy a Unicomp. It has great tactile and audio feedback. You should use this keyboard on a PC running the almost-current copy of Windows and the almost-current copy of Microsoft Word—the only word processing program you should even attempt to use if you plan to publish.

The wine guy writer (me) from the night before eventually has dinner and goes to bed and wakes up in the morning after REM sleep. Some great ideas from the night before are refreshed and made ready to go. I have learned that I had better check all the work from the day before which was produced rapid fire.

When I change from rapid-fire writer to editor in the morning, I find a lot of mistakes that I missed while I was writing. Of course I am both guys but the half day (nighttime) that passes makes it seem like I am editing somebody else's work and so I get almost all of the editing changes in just one extra pass over the work of the day before.

Let me go over this again. When I read the stuff from the prior day, especially that which was written rapid-fire by the wine guy, I find extremely insightful thought that I enjoy very much but there is often poor sentence structure and some poor grammar use. So, I spend my first half hour of each writing day reviewing this work and making corrections before I go on again with creative writing.

I love creative writing immensely. Both me's in the process, the wine guy and the editor still may miss some things that are not at first obvious. Eventually, both of us, who are both me, create a book that we think is worthy of publication. Most errors of this kind will be caught in final edit. In my opinion few books are ever 100% perfect but we all should try to make ours as perfect as possible.

Besides all the formatting steps that are needed, in the proofing area, a third me, the final editor, does not believe that either of the two other guys know what they are doing. So the third *I, the real me in me,* reviews the whole thing in multiple ways. When the book is finished, I run through the WORD Spell checker and it shows me grammar issues and spelling issues that I had not seen despite my other reviews.

Side note; do not use an old version of Word. Most older versions are not as good at finding the nuances that are problems that will annoy you if your book is printed and it includes these issues!

As much as I want to rush through the spell and grammar check invoked via the Word Review Tab, I know that the third I in me, must take my time or I will miss the subtleties that Word recommends that can change the perfection of the writing. So I take my time and methodically go through each page and I reflect and make changes as the process goes on.

I could never have caught all of these little things if I had written by hand and hired a typist. The interaction with the machine makes one a better writer in today's world. Every so often, I must completely rewrite a paragraph during this edit if it simply does not make sense. Yes, that does happen!

After I feel OK with the spell check, I do my final edit for my manuscript. In recent years, I have just one Word file. In prior years to make up for word tools that I did not know how to use. I would create two files. One file was for what I call the front matter and I created another word document for the main book.

We will get to all of this. After all, I just turned in my eighty-third book (in 2020, I am now at 231). So, I know how to get this stuff to the marketplace but as I get older, I produce much more readable and much more enjoyable books. I hope overall, this book will tell you why!

So, the next big step is to read the book. Some pages or chapters I read very slowly because they are substantial and written well, and other areas are not done as well. I need to discuss these as in the other edits, I sometimes presume things are right and a I go quickly. In my second edit I skip things believing they are perfect (not a good idea). Though I hope to edit everything well, poorly written stuff is a bore even if I write it and I find myself not looking as intensely for errors in areas that I am not enjoying in my reading.

My advice which I do follow sometimes when perfection is more important than at other times, is to put the book down for a few weeks and sometimes months and bring in the fourth me, the re-editor, who typically finds the whole book enjoyable and has the patience to edit by reading the text very closely. The better the end product of a book, the more all four me's are involved in making it perfect.

Yet, as previously noted, the truth is that no book is ever perfect.

As a professor for innumerable years, I must read books from cover to cover before I adopt them for a course and permit my students to read them. Being a tech writer for many years, I often smile when I see a mistake from the tech pros in their prose.

It is most often in non-essential areas but even the best of the best make mistakes. Proofing one's own book is a means of saving a lot of needed cash, especially if the first book does not sell well. Any method that gets you to complete your first work is a better deal than you ever thinking that you cannot afford to write. My objective is always to produce a book which costs me nothing. Hold on and we will eventually get to that in this book.

Chapter 3 Structuring Your Book for Publishing

Some helpful structuring tid-bits

To help you in structuring your book for publishing, I am including the how-to for two sections (front matter and main book) in one document. As noted previously, with my former book printer, I normally would submit two files to the printing company. One would be for the front matter (before page 1) and the other would be for the book per se, including the index if the type of book I was writing, such as tech books, required it.

When I got better with Word over time, I learned to love the table of contents creator. By using a different author-created Word style for the chapter heading, which in my books, I create as **ChapterHead**. *I can ask Word to create a table of contents automagically for me. By the way, Word creates a TOC that Kindle applies to its E-books so little work needs to be done to create a Kindle version of a submitted word manuscript. At one time, I redid my manuscripts for Kindle. Not any more.*

When I wrote this set of instructions originally five years or more ago I cautioned my students and the faculty who were interested in learning how to publish to "Pardon spelling because I am going to whip through this because I promised it to you." I also promised that I would do more: "I will send you the cover work for my new book if you want it." The cover printout is included in the next chapter.

This information can serve as a discussion point and reference for you to begin writing your own book or when you have a very large paper and need about 20 copies in a bound form., you can get a nice cover designed for a book for about $100 to $150. Additionally, it would cost about $4.00 per book for 20 books from a print on demand printer such as Offset Paperback (OPM) in Laflin, PA. http://www.beprintersamerica.com/OPM/ContactUs.aspx. These are rough ball parks. My point is you won't go broke.

Check out www.letsgopublish for my books as well as www.amazon.com/author/brianwkelly. Additionally, all my recent books are orderable at this last link. You can also see all my covers— some professionally designed and some use covers created by the COVERS CREATOR tool.

Again, when I would submit a book to OPM Printers prior to 2016, I would provide them with at least two PDF files. PDF files can be produced directly from Word or with Adobe Acrobat or CutePDF or other programs. I use CutePDF to create a PDF from each MS Word document. Today I sometimes use the innate create pdf capability in Word called Microsoft Print to PDF. Other than to create a Kindle ebook, most printing shops want a pdf not a Word version of your manuscript.

As noted, one file can be front matter—the material before page 1 of the book. The second file is the main book from start to finish including the index and an advertisements page for Lets Go Publish (other books of mine).

Use Amazon's KDP for your self-publishing

In 2016, at the urging of my good friend Paul Harkins, still using my Lets Go Publish! Imprint, I experimented with CreateSpace and eventually began to use this great service for most of my printing and publishing work. After Amazon bought CreateSpace, I now use Amazon KDP printing.

I have updated the rest of this book to show how the Amazon KDP Print works with authors to get books printed. When I first self-published using the available tools it was a tool called *CreateSpace*, which is no longer available even though there are entrails of it still searchable on the Internet.

The Book I wrote was titled *How to Write Your First Book and Publish It Using CreateSpace* .The book from back then is still available but this book is the one you should use today since Amazon no longer supports the CreateSpace tools. It's title as you know is *How to Write Your First Book and Publish It Using Amazon's KDP.*

To get going, Type in ***self publishing on Amazon*** to find out where the Amazon tools are that we will use in this book. You will get to a page that gives you the following information:

Self-publish eBooks and paperbacks for free with Kindle Direct Publishing (KDP), and reach millions of readers on Amazon.
Get to market fast. Publishing takes less than 5 minutes and your book appears on Kindle stores worldwide within 24-48 hours.

Make more money. Earn up to 70% royalty on sales to customers in the US, Canada, UK, Germany, India, France, Italy, Spain, Japan, Brazil, Mexico, Australia and more. Enroll in KDP Select and earn more money through Kindle Unlimited and the Kindle Owners' Lending Library.

Keep control. Keep control of your rights and set your own list prices. Make changes to your books at any time.

Publish in digital and print. Publish Kindle eBooks and paperbacks for free on KDP.

Get started today! Self-publish with KDP for free.

To see more, click on the next sentence ***Learn how easy it is.***

Once you click, Amazon explains its KDP Print process to you and takes you on a journey that it hopes will make a published author out of you. You will see:

Prepare, Publish, Promote, Getting Started

Getting Started

Amazon writes: *You just finished writing the next hit romance novel. Or maybe a memoir destined for the big screen. Or perhaps the first volume of a gripping fantasy series. Now you've decided to self-publish your book on KDP, which lets you publish both eBooks and paperbacks.*
How do you want to start?

1. Step-by-step guidance. For an end-to-end guide with insider tips for self-publishing on Amazon, try the link--**KDP Jumpstart**.

2. Learn on your own. Use our link--**self-guided resources** to get started publishing eBooks and paperbacks.

3. KDP University. For a comprehensive suite of resources designed to help you take your best book to market, visit--**KDP University.**

4. Frequently asked questions. See a --**List of common questions** from authors getting started on KDP.

5. Want an overview of the KDP website, as well as publishing tools and marketing tips? See our **Getting Started with KDP video.**

For now, why don't you find your writing PC and catch up to this spot in the book by taking the actions on the Amazon KDP Getting Started Pag starting with List item #1 and going until you finish looking at #5.
r :

Unlike when I worked with OPM, in which I separated the front matter from the main body in the book, Amazon KDP's requirements were for each book submission to be in one file. After writing so many book using various versions of Microsoft Word, I was able to figure out what I needed to do in order to combine the front matter with the main book. It was not hard at all.

Once I began to use word, I learned that I had to know more than in other word processors I had used. For example, to be able to publish with word, I had to learn how to create each chapter in its own section. Sections are vital to a lot of things in publishing your book with word, so let's define the term right below:

Sections are subdivisions of a document. Once a document is divided into sections, you can make formatting changes that apply only to one section. For instance, you can change the page orientation or the number of columns for just one section. Sections are separated with section breaks.

When I type a book with Word, I place one chapter in one book section. In word, a section is a very formal notion. I also start each chapter on an odd page. Most authors use this rule. I like how the completed book looks with new chapters beginning only on the right side page.

It is recommended to start all new chapters on what is called the recto page of a manuscript, as it establishes a predictable flow for the reader to follow. The resulting occasional blank pages on the left side of the fold are actually a part of establishing this rhythm, making the divisions between chapters even more distinct. This recommendation is listed in rule 1.48 of the Chicago Manual of Style.

At am earlier point in my writing and publishing career, I used both OPM and KDP depending on whether I wanted to sell the books on my sales site, www.bookhawkers.com or not. BookHawkers is now defunct but I may resuscitate it in the future.

My point is that once I switched to the one file / one full book document approach, which I would recommend to all new book authors, I no longer use the two-file method. I have submitted work with one file to OPM and they work with it just as easily as when I separated the front matter from the main text.

Regardless of whether the front matter is contained in its own file or as part of a comprehensive one-document book file, I structure each book the same.

The front matter matters:

I have my own style which includes the same parts that most authors and publishers include in their front matter. In one of my books, you will typically find the sections outlined below. As you can see, the parts of the front matter are generally described.

Later in this chapter, I will show a full example and discuss each page's components in better detail. For now, let's assume that the manuscript has no page numbers. Let's start right with the first page (AKA page one) and continue to the end of the front matter.

First Page—In my books, on the first page, I introduce the book. I may use a picture of the book or another picture and/or, I use descriptive text.

Second Page—inside front page has copious **publisher information**

Page 3 I include the Lets Go Publish **Logo**

Page 5—I use this for the book's **dedication**.

Page 7 I use this for **acknowledgments**. My acknowledgments were once a litany of family and friends who enjoy seeing their names in print but I now put the litany of thank-you's on the web)

If more than two pages are used for any front matter section the page #s in this front matter guide would change. Some Sections are not included in every book.

Page 9 Here is where I would include one to several pages of free form **references** and a description of why. This is not standard but it saves me in certain books from using ibid, and op.cit., and footnotes and a bibliography. I don't write really formal books so this gets me past a big unnecessary hurdle. It works for me.

Page 11—If I include a **foreword**, it goes here. It follows acknowledgments. A Book Foreword is a short essay about your book written by a third party. It gives the reader a reason why they should read your book

Page 13—A **preface** is a short essay about your book either written by you or somebody affiliated with your work such as an editor.

Page 15—A **table of contents at a glance** is a one line summary of Chapters and/or Sections)

Page 17—A **table of contents (toc)** is somewhat self-explanatory. This one if present is a detailed TOC with heads and subheads. My Tech books' TOCs are often huge. I like to use multiple levels of heads to break up text in tech books. I use all of these as a quasi-book-outline.

When you write your book, the more complex the book, the more you will want to use heads and subheads to mimic the outline of the book. I will show you what typical text might be found at various levels of heading. When I wrote tech books, this was much more important than now as I write mostly patriotic, sports, and political books.

The Table of contents needs to be built when editing the main book file if you use the two document approach. Then, it must be copied into the Front-Matter document file via copy and paste.
When you use the one document book file approach, create the TOC within the document where you plan to place it in the front matter.

Page 19—An optional section called a**bout the author** is a later part of the front matter often shows a picture of the author as well as a few paragraphs of biographical information.

Now, let us discuss heading levels; how to create them; and then examine how the Word table of contents generator does its job.

Differentiating headings by level

Suppose I want this to be head level 1, which after Chapter Headings is the most important heading, aka, the top level heading.

Head1 (Heading) Level 1 Highlighted in image below

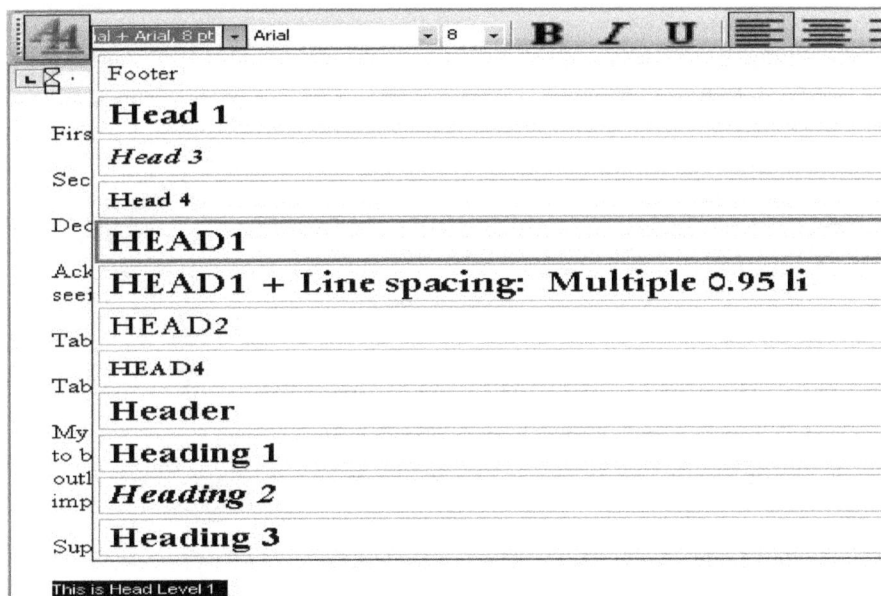

A word look at the heading levels in a document

Look at the text highlighted above in the graphic. It is very small and looks like a black band at the bottom. We will make this text into Head Level 1. Highlight your text as above and bring down the styles window as shown above in the graphic. Then, pick Head1 by selecting it with the mouse.

In newer versions of Word, such as Word 2013, the Styles Window is selected from the Home Tab and it appears as follows:

Clipboard ⌟   Fon

🛈 GET THE NEW OFFICE It's o

Styles   ▾ ✕

eight + Line spacing: Multip	
eight + Line spacing: Multip	
eight + Times New Roman,	
eight + Times New Roman,	
eight + Times New Roman,	
eight + Times New Roman,	
eight + Times New Roman,	
eudoraheader	a
FollowedHyperlink	a
Footer	¶
Head 1	¶
Head 3	¶a
Head 4	¶
HEAD1	¶a
HEAD1 + Line spacing: Mul	
Head2	¶
HEAD2	¶a
Head2 + Border: : (No bord	
HEAD4	¶
Header	¶
Heading 1	¶
Heading 2	¶
Heading 3	¶

I had previously created word style Head 1. When you select this style, the text will be formatted as a level 1 header which means it is important and bigger text. Level 2 is defined as smaller text and would be one level less important. In this document, I created a style called Chapter Head as most important with the biggest font size. Here are these three examples on the next page.

Chapter 1 Welcome to Chapter 1

Head 1 Welcome to Head 1

Head 2 Welcome to Head 2

By using captions such as these, you get to outline your book as you are writing it and Word will automatically create your table of contents for you as if it is a complete outline.

That was pretty quick so let's do it again

To select a set of text to be a specific level of head, there are steps to take as we have already discussed.

Suppose the text we wish to use is what we will actually do below in this document:

Insert / Reference / Index and Tables

Let's say we want this text to be text level 1. To do this we highlight the text as follows:

Insert / Reference / Index and Tables

Then, we pick Head1 and the header for the next section at Level 1 will look like:

Insert / Reference / Index and Tables

In newer Windows and Windows 10 OS, we would do as follows:

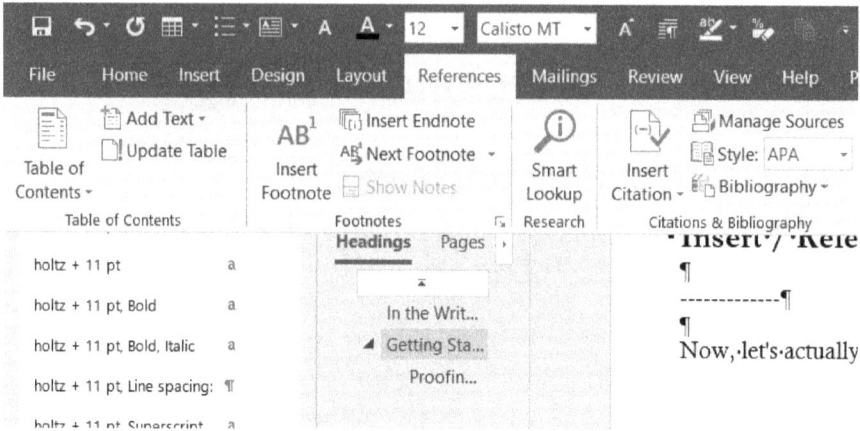

Click on Refences, and then select Table of Contents. After the next prompt, the system will go ahead and create a table of contents. For you right at that place in the document. Neat? You bet!

Now, let's do it again after selecting that level 1 text in our document as below:

Insert / Reference / Index and Tables

After we have created our chapter heads, level 1 through level 4 heads as we write the book, we can create the table of contents for this book. First we must open the main book file. We want the TOC creator to build us a detailed table of contents from the main book material. If the front matter is in the same file and it had heading levels that we wish to use, this process will accommodate them. If we are using two files then we would copy the TOC to the Front Matter file after table-of-contents (TOC) creation.

To create the TOC when editing the main book file, click the following:

Insert / Reference / Index and Tables   or
Reference / Table of Contents

In Widows 2013, Reference is already a main so we do not need to start with insert. The action above will poof create your table of contents at wherever in the book you are positioned.

If you are in the back of the book after all text in the main book, it will go there. This makes sense only for the two file system. You would then copy this TOC to its own file to pretty it up and then copy the edited version to the front matter right into the Table of Contents Section. This will all make more sense when we get into the examples in Chapter 5.

I have already described the fact that I generate my TOC automatically with Word by using Head levels that I apply to the various headers when I write the book. You will see the HEAD levels in the main book part of the one file or the main book file in a two-file scenario. From this point on, I will no longer discuss the two-file approach.

I use Roman Numeral page numbering for the front matter and use regular Arabic (US) numbers in the main document.

Creating an Index

In tech books, it is good to have an index so that a geek looking for a quick way to do something does not have to amble through the table of contents or leaf through the book to scan for ext.

You can automatically create an index in a similar way to creating a table of contents. Once the book is done, most authors desiring to have an index, walk through the text in their entire document and mark items to be included in the index. The process remembers what page the ext is on and creates a separate file when you are done that most authors would copy to the back of the book where they like to place the index.

When the auto-index creator does its job, it takes the word or phrase and its page # and places it in the index and then later, it creates the index in alphabetical sequence.

The first step is to mark the words in the document. You mark words for inclusion in the index by highlighting the word or phrase and then clicking on Mark Index. A box then appears as shown on the next page:

Mark Index Entry   ?   ✕

Index

Main entry: Mark Index

Subentry:

Options

○ Cross-reference: See

● Current page

○ Page range

  Bookmark:

Page number format

☐ Bold

☐ Italic

This dialog box stays open so that you can mark multiple index entries.

[Mark]   [Mark All]   [Cancel]

You would click the Mark button for one index occurrence or click on the Mark All button to pick all occurrences of the two words Mark Index every place it appears in the document. After selecting the word and marking it, it is ready to be included in the index. If you display

codes ¶ next to the words Mark Index above, you would see the index code as follows: { XE "Mark Index" } s

If you mark items to be in the index, the index creation for the back of the book is similar to the Table of Contents creation. This is just a simple summary about how word does its tricks. My solid advice it to take a class at a Community College or a self-study to learn MS Word. It will help make you a better author

To create an index after all your words are marked, position yourself in the book where you want the index created and pick the reference tab and then on the right hand side click on Insert Index. Poof! The index will appear in your book. It is like magic

Here is a reference on how to get an index created if your book needs an index. My later books do not need an index as they are reading books and not reference books. Here is how to get that done. It is fairly straight forward and saves an awful lot of work. Take the link

https://support.microsoft.com/en-us/kb/212346

In summary, I generate the index automatically by marking words in the book and then telling Word to create an index and then I reformat the Index into multiple columns in the main file. The above link will show you how to do that. I wait until the book is done since page numbers can get messed up if text is added after the index is created. I usually end the front matter with the Preface or the About the Author Section.

In this book manuscript, I use an MS section break. (Insert Break / odd Page) for each section or chapter. Sometimes I write the Preface and sometimes the publisher does (In both cases I include the text into the front matter.). If somebody writes a prologue or a foreword, you would put it before the preface.

I use Section breaks for each Chapter.

Each Chapter has its own main heading and starts on an odd page. I use odd and even page headers. The even page header stays the same with the book name throughout the book. The odd page, I change by creating an odd (MS-Word) section break for each chapter.

I use fairly standard style for my Chapters with a larger Font for the Chapter Title followed by about six spaces. I always have a first HEAD level to make the First Chapter Page look important.

I like using Headers as they make the book easier to read. Watch widow and orphan headers. If you do not know what they are, please study this reference:

http://word.tips.net/T001149_Controlling_Widows_and_Orphans.html

You can use paragraph control to keep header lines with text. I do that all the time to avoid the widow / orphan problem with headers.

For example highlight the header or picture caption and the picture or the next paragraph after the header, then click

Format / Paragraph / Line & Page breaks / and check the keep with next box.

Class 1 Formatting Picture to Stay with the Caption

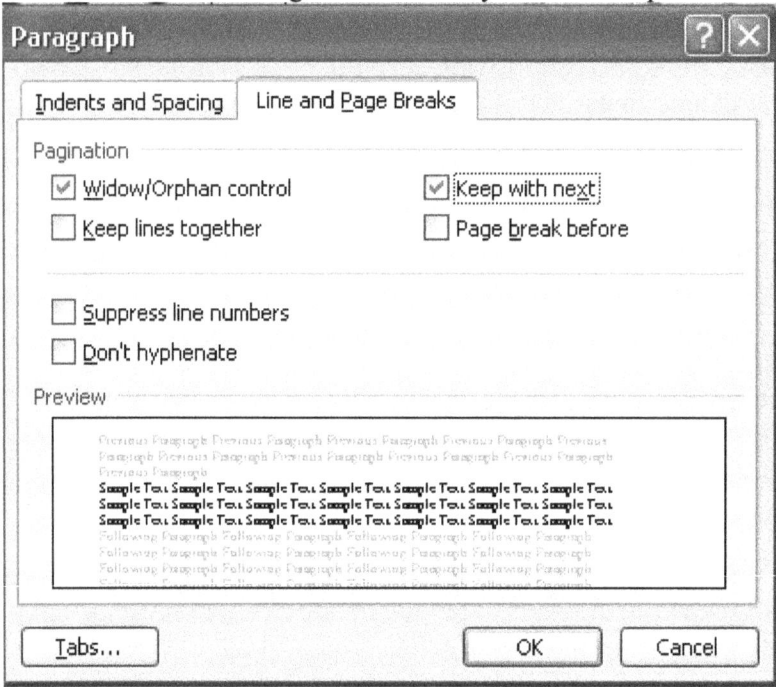

First highlight just the caption and change it to italic (my preference)

Then highlight the caption and the picture

Format / Paragraph / Indents and Spacing / Centered.

This centers the picture and the caption.

Then, highlight again and

Format / Paragraph / Line & Page breaks / and check the keep with next box.

This prevents the caption from being on one page and the picture on another

I create a separate odd section break at the end of the book for the index and then on the next even page, I put the Lets Go Publish Advertising page or pages -- always on the last page (even) or set of pages of the book.

This material is in this sample document at the end. When everything is finished, I create a PDF of the entire book using either Acrobat or CutePDF (free download) or the Microsoft *Print to PDF* facility as follows:

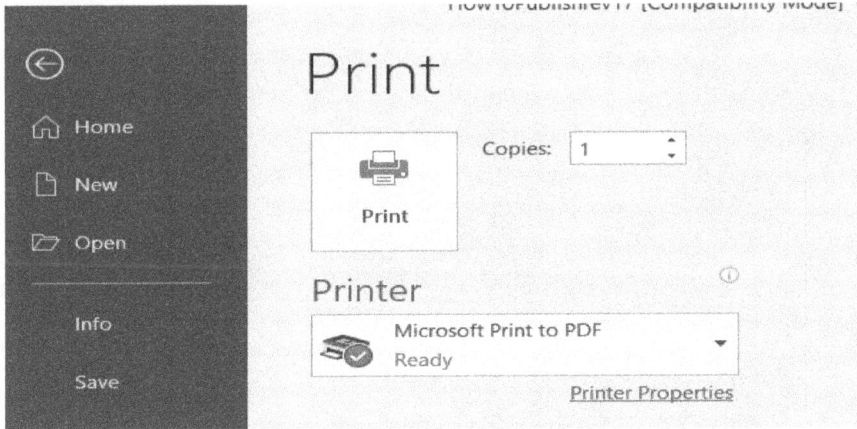

I review page by page the PDF to make sure the formatting is correct. Then I email the file to the printer or I begin the Amazon KDF print creation process. You can download a free PDF creator at

http://www.cutepdf.com/Products/CutePDF/writer.asp

When everything is finished, using the one document per book system, I create one pdf of the entire book using either Acrobat or CutePDF (free download) and I review page by page the pdf front matter and the book all at once to make sure the formatting is correct. Then I email the one file to the printer.

When using Amazon's KDP, the pdf file gets uploaded during the book publishing process. We discuss how to do this in later chapters. ---------

Chapter 4 Your Book Cover

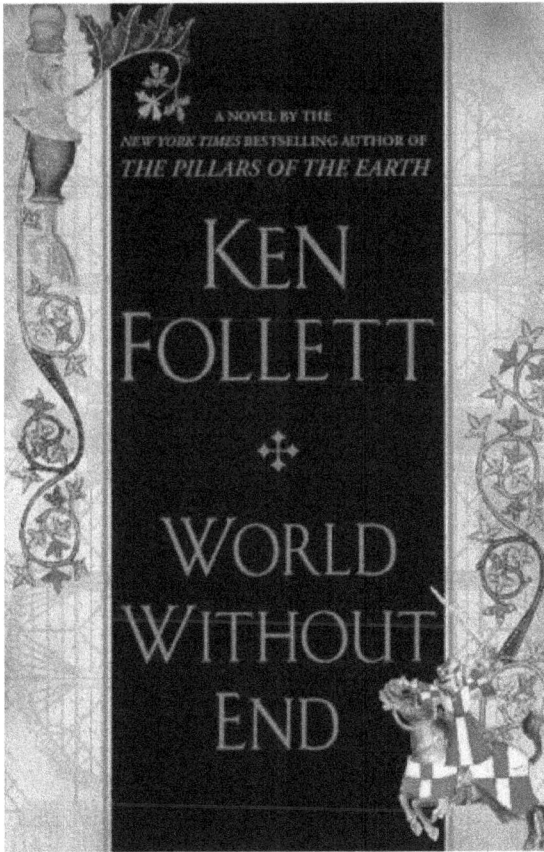

Do people buy books by their cover?

I do think so!

Make sure your cover is attractive or nobody will want your book.

When I know about how many pages I want in a book (or as I work on it how many pages I think it will be), if my cover in my mind will be complicated, I begin to work with my cover designer, Michele Thomas. I normally have some ideas or I look books up on Amazon or other sites to check out options and get a general idea of what might be a good overall look for a certain book. I used the Ken Follett book on the prior page for example as a book cover design guide.

I send Michele a look that I like and then I tell her about what text or other graphics I may want on the front and the back cover. I create all of the cover text. My front covers have always been exceptionally nice but for this new book that I was working on in 2007 or so, I wanted something different.

My book title was *Taxation Without Representation.* I first looked for a book title that contained the word *Without.* I found *World Without End.* Go ahead and google it. I then found some coin images and some clip-art stamps with Uncle Sam and a pattern and I sent it all to Michele to get a rough cut that I used in my cover. Almost every time Michele sends me a rough cut it is good enough for final copy unless I have made a mistake.

See the sample cover I sent to Michele above (Follett):

The back cover text for the taxation book originally was too small for the space available for example, so she sent it back to me and I re-edited the cover text and reduced the number of words and sent the new version back to Michele, my cover designer.
.
The finished cover I show for this book may give you an idea on what is needed and the fact that it is an iterative process.

Hope this helps

The front matter file is exact and the main book file which we will show later is a stripped down version to show the things I discussed above about front matter and chapter headings etc..

Hope this all makes sense.
This ends the note to my students and faculty. Here is what the cover looks like now in its third version of this 2008 best seller. On the first page of this chapter, is one of the book designs *World Without End* that I had given my book cover designer.

I loved this design. My designer, Michele Thomas takes a good idea and makes it even better. Here is her rendition of this cover for the third edition of my Taxation W/O Representation Book.

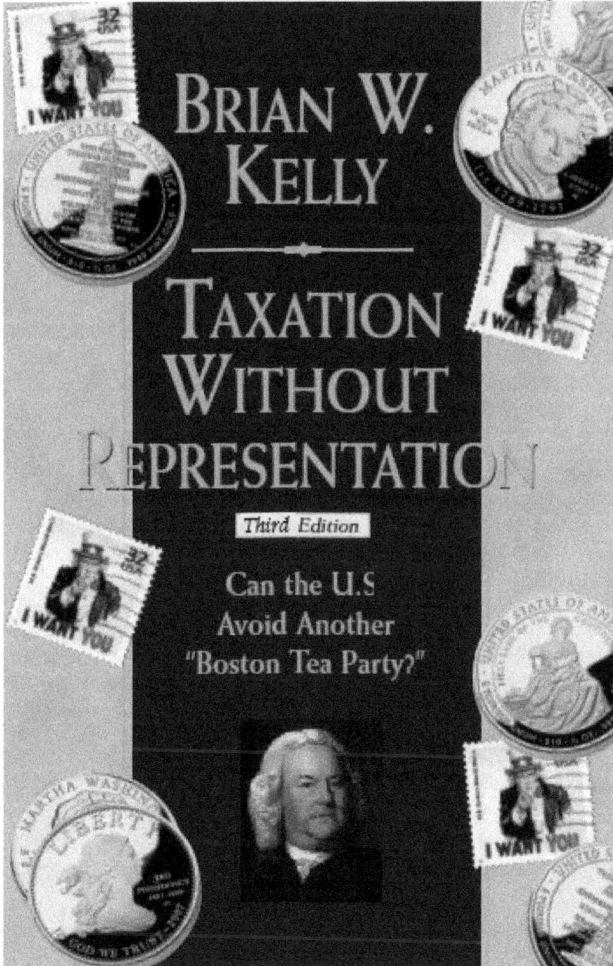

The back of the book is also a feature of a great book designer's efforts. Remember when Michele did this original design, I was a lot younger. The book price is now $17.95 and $2.99 on Kindle. Here is the back cover:

Chapter 5 A look at the Parts of a Book by Example

Page 1 Sample

LETS GO United States of America!

Taxation
Without
Representation

Can the U.S. Avoid Another "Boston Tea Party?"

This book relies on the Constitution, the founding documents, Articles of Association, Declaration of Rights and Grievances, Declaration of Independence, and the Bill of Rights (the text of each is included in our appendices) as the basis for the conclusions made herein. Taxation Without Representation unearths and explores a massive dilemma for U.S. Citizens. We began without representation. Then, the Colonies fought a war of independence to acquire representation. Now, our beloved representatives have fallen for the candy coated wiles of the new kids on the block--obscenely rich mega-corporations. This offers a walk-though through on how our government once was, how it improved, and how it again eroded and regressed to its oppressive roots. The book highlights the major issues affecting the American worker, particularly the wholesale exportation of jobs to legal and illegal foreign nationals. The book also discusses how both political parties are preventing independent candidates from appearing on ballots and the problems presented by voting machines surreptitiously designed with technology that enables an interested party's surrogates to manipulate and even override the people's will. Our representative democracy is definitely in trouble. This book offers a number of unique solutions to help get us back on track. Enjoy.

LETS GO PUBLISH

BRIAN W. KELLY

Let's start with how a Page 1 should look

See above. While most readers try ferociously to skip the introductions (front matter material) in books and go right to the preface or chapter 1, nonetheless, front matter is very necessary to a book for its completeness.

Start off your first page with a huge title and a smaller subtitle area.

Page 1 should be attractive or at least tell the book story in the fewest words possible. It should clearly identify that the book cover represents the book contents. Either I put a nice picture here or a shaded text area that is much shorter than the Preface but contains preface and back book cover type material.

In your book, make sure that Page 1 looks good. Find books that you have seen in the past and look to see if there are notions that you would like to have on page 1 of your book. Those that I picked for Taxation Without Representation are shown on the next page.

Since my publishing company is Lets Go Publish!, I put a little phrase on the top of the first page in all of my early books that brought the title of the book together with the publishing company. As you can see, this is *Lets Go United States of America*. It is followed by the Title and subtitle. Then I use a shaded area to give a brief abstract of the book. At the bottom, I put the company logo and my name as the author. It is shown on the next page:

On a following page is page 2 also known as the Publisher's page. Everybody's publisher page looks different. This is mine. I created it for my first book and fine-tuned it. What you see is what it looked like in 2008. It does not look much different today. As you can see, I start with the copyright and then the book title and subtitle.

Following this I have a rights section which reads as follows:

All rights reserved: No part of this book may be reproduced or transmitted in any form, or by any means, electronic or mechanical, including photocopying, recording, scanning, faxing, or by any information storage and retrieval system, without permission from the publisher, LETS GO PUBLISH, in writing.

After this is the Disclaimer which basically says that I did my best and when you read this, it may not be 100% correct. You put this in to avoid lawsuits. Following the Disclaimer, I put a blurb about Trademarks followed by Referenced Material as I do not copy material without permission or at least reference to the source.

Disclaimer: Though judicious care was taken throughout the writing and the publication of this work that the information contained herein is accurate, there is no expressed or implied warranty that all information in this book is 100% correct. Therefore, neither LETS GO PUBLISH, nor the author accepts liability for any use of this work.

Trademarks: A number of products and names referenced in this book are trade names and trademarks of their respective companies.

Referenced Material : *The information in this book has been obtained through personal and third party observations, interviews, and copious research and analysis. Where unique information has been provided or extracted from other sources, those sources are acknowledged within the text of the book itself or at the end of the chapter in the Sources Section. Thus, there are no formal footnotes nor is there a bibliography section. Any picture that does not have a source was taken from various sites on the Internet with no credit attached. If any resource owner would like credit in the next printing, please email the publisher.*

The rest of the information on the publisher's page is pretty self-explanatory except for the numbers 10,9, 8…1

Each printing of the book, I remove a number So that printing #2 would be designated by the lack of a number 1.

On Page 3, I like to place the Lets Go Publish! Logo. It is my company.

On Page 5 is a very nice Dedication to my wife

On Page 7 is the beginning of what once was a twenty page acknowledgment set. I took this out and put it on the web when I began to write for CreateSpace Publishing as there is a healthy charge for printed pages. All of the acknowledgments still exist. Go to www.letsgopublish.com and from the main menu, pick Acknowledgments from the left column of the site

In this book, I have the table of contents before the preface and there is no *about the author* section.

On Page 11, I show the Table of Contents which is basically the section / chapter headings.

On Page 13, we show the full table of contents with all subheadings included. This section was edited in a separate file to achieve the look.

The Preface comes after the TOC. Here are some pages if the front matter for your review:

Page 2 Sample Publisher's Page

Copyright © 2008, Brian W. Kelly
Taxation without Representation   Author Brian W. Kelly
Can the U.S. Avoid Another "Boston Tea Party"?

All rights reserved: No part of this book may be reproduced or transmitted in any form, or by any means, electronic or mechanical, including photocopying, recording, scanning, faxing, or by any information storage and retrieval system, without permission from the publisher, LETS GO PUBLISH, in writing.

Disclaimer: Though judicious care was taken throughout the writing and the publication of this work that the information contained herein is accurate, there is no expressed or implied warranty that all information in this book is 100% correct. Therefore, neither LETS GO PUBLISH, nor the author accepts liability for any use of this work.

Trademarks: A number of products and names referenced in this book are trade names and trademarks of their respective companies.

Referenced Material : *The information in this book has been obtained through personal and third party observations, interviews, and copious research and analysis. Where unique information has been provided or extracted from other sources, those sources are acknowledged within the text of the book itself or at the end of the chapter in the Sources Section. Thus, there are no formal footnotes nor is there a bibliography section. Any picture that does not have a source was taken from various sites on the Internet with no credit attached. If any resource owner would like credit in the next printing, please email the publisher.*

Published by: LETS GO PUBLISH!
Publisher: Joseph J. McDonald,   **Editor:** Brian P. Kelly
                     P.O Box 834
                     Scranton, PA 18505
                     imac160@verizon.net
                     www.letsgopublish.com

Library of Congress Copyright Information Pending

Book Cover Design by Michele Thomas, Editing by Brian P. Kelly

ISBN Information: The International Standard Book Number (ISBN) is a unique machine-readable identification number, which marks any book unmistakably. The ISBN is the clear standard in the book industry. 159 countries and territories are officially ISBN members. The Official ISBN For this book is on the outside cover:

ISBN Number is on outside cover: **978-0-9802132-0-1**

The price for this work is :   **$17.95 USD**

10   9   8   7   6   5   4   3   2   1

Logo Sample Page 3

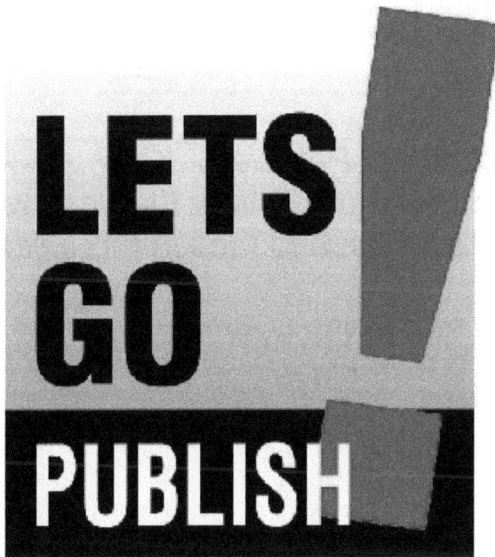

Dedication Sample Page 5

Dedication

I dedicate this book to Patricia A. Kelly, my wonderful wife. You have endured more writing than any wonderful lady should ever have to face in three lifetimes.

You make everything better!
I love you Pat!

Acknowledgments Sample Page 7

Acknowledgments

I would like to thank many, many people for helping me in this effort.

I would first like to thank my immediate family, starting with my lovely and dear wife, Patricia. Again, as I offer in all my books, my Pat is number one. You are the first person I see every day and the last one I see at night and I am jealous of the time in between. We're going on forty years together and it seems like yesterday that we met. What a life! And, you are so wonderful to all of the family, taking care of the problems that seem to come up all the time. Even the dog (Bennie) and the cat (Buddie) can't get by a day without you. Thank you a zillion plus the largest number in the world. You are my beauty and when you announce yourself after coming in from school, I can't wait to see you. I often take the time to just sneak a peek at you and I don't even tell you. I hear you buzzing around the house as I write and it just tickles me. Your daddy, Smokey, became a best friend to me and I loved how he always called you his little girl Packy. The "Smoke" and the "Skip" are now with the Angels but the memories are forever. I do smile just thinking of you and I love you dearly. Thank you Packy for all you do to keep me and our whole family well and mostly, thank you for just being you.

I would also like to thank my twenty-three year-old daughter, Katie, who has been Daddy's little girl now for all of her 23 years. You are one of the kindest people in the whole world. I know that you have had your struggles but you are facing things today and mowing them down. I am very proud of you and even more proud as you took me for Christmas dinner with your clients, who are not as fortunate in life as most. How wonderful it was watching my little girl offering kindness and taking care of people who really need you. You are just wonderful. Just the other day when you were ill along with all the clients and you stayed to clean up the problem, your co-worker told your mom what a nice person you are and how fortunate she is to work with you. Whenever I meet those who know you, for the first time, they can't wait to tell me what a sweetheart you are. I am also very proud of all those A's you are getting in college, you sharpie. Thank you for your help and please know that you will always be Daddy's Little Girl. I love you very much.

Thanks also go out to my twenty-six-year-old son, Michael, who is in his last semester of Law School. You finished the Fall Semester and I got to enjoy your company over the holidays. Now, you are on your way, like your big brother to being a lawyer. I'll stay out of trouble 'til you can both help me. It was great this past summer Michael that you interned with one of the most respected Law Firms in Northeastern Pennsylvania, Borland and Borland. The Borlands really liked you and your work. It's nice to see that big heart of yours in action Mike. You are a good son and it is to your credit that you have not taken the easy way out of certain situations. I'm proud of that big heart and my wonderful good son.

Thank you also to my tall and handsome twenty-seven year-old son, Brian, who knocked 'em dead in Law School and graduated Magna Cum Laude and then killed the BAR exam. You were an essential ingredient in helping me pull this work together. You are a phenomenal writer. When I was flat on knowing how to say something, you wrote exactly what I would have written if I were given your wonderful talents. I am glad the migraines are settling down now. I could not have done this work without you, my editor in chief. I almost don't want you going back to

Table of Contents Glance Sample Page 9

Table of Contents at a Glance

Part I: The Problem 1
Chapter 1 We Get the Government We Deserve................................. 1
Chapter 2 Too Many Honorables 19
Chapter 3: Taxes, Taxes, and More Taxes..................................... 55
Chapter 4 The American Fight - Liberty & Rep. Govt. 73
Chapter 5 The Forming of the U.S. Government 101

Part II How Did It Get This Bad? 115
Chapter 6 Corporate Power & New Robber Barons 115
Chapter 7 Unions Meet the Robber Baron Challenge........................ 149
Chapter 8 Worker Visas Take Many American Jobs 173
Chapter 9 Offshoring: Bad for America...................................... 197
Chapter 10 AWOL Again on Illegal Aliens 237
Chapter 11 Theft-Proofing Election Process.................................. 309

Part III A Few Silver Bullets!... 355
Chapter 12 General Solutions-- Future of the U. S. 355
Chapter 13 Silver Bullet for Taxes & More Taxes 371
Chapter 14 Silver Bullets for Corporations, Unions, |
            Visas, and Offshoring... 379
Chapter 15 Silver Bullet for Illegal Aliens 413

Appendix A The Declaration of Rights and Grievances 449
Appendix B The Articles of Association 455
Appendix C The Declaration of Independence 461
Appendix D The Articles of Confederation.................................. 467
Appendix E The Constitution of the U.S.A. 477
Appendix F The Bill of Rights & Amendments 491
Appendix G Constitutional Amendments Not Ratified........................ 505
Appendix H American Essays from Thomas Dawson.......................... 509
      Illegal Aliens and Immigration 511
      All Immigration Problems Solved 516
      Labor Arbitrage? Better Known as Cheap Labor 519
      Coin of the Realm.. 523

Table of Contents Sample Pages

Table of Contents

Part I: The Problem...1

Chapter 1 We Get the Government We Deserve.....................1
America Is a Representative Democracy?.................................. 1
It's Time to Fire Them!... 3
Benign Oligarchy Can Use Some Direct Democracy 8
Checks and Balances Aren't Working 9

Chapter 2 Too Many Honorables.. 19
The Issues of Today.. 19
The Honorable Congressman from Blankety Blank 22
A Method to Solve Problems 23
But Is Puffery Really The Problem? 42
Civics Lesson.. 44
Constitutional Democracy and Other Political Regimes 46

Chapter 3: Taxes, Taxes, and More Taxes............................... 55
Everything Costs Money.. 55
Government's Share of Your Income Is Increasing.................... 56
State Taxes... 59
Local Taxes 60
Federal Taxes.. 61
Send In What You Want? 62

Chapter 4 The American Fight for Liberty and Representative Government..73
Representative Democracy Revisited..................................... 73
Columbus, Vespucci, de León, & Cabot.................................. 73
The House of Representatives 77
The Problem With Colonial Suffrage 79
Illegal Taxation.. 84
The Beginning of the American Revolution 90
War Justification: 95
Cornwallis Surrenders 96

Chapter 5 The Forming of the U. S. Government.................. 101
Representation at All Levels.. 101
United States Declaration of Independence 103
Articles of Confederation 104
The Constitution of the United States of America.................... 106
The Law of the Land 107

Part II How Did It Get This Bad?......................................115

Chapter 6 Rise of Corporate Power -The New Robber Barons 115
The Union is Not Perfect.. 115
Money, Corporations and the Owner Class................................... 117
The Robber Barons Are Back... 121
John Edwards Has It 100% Right.. 124
Time for a Structural Change... 125
The Plight of the Worker.. 134

Chapter 7 Countervailing Power: Unions Meet the Robber Baron Challenge.. 149
The Rise Of Powerful Labor Unions.. 150
Strikes Often Turn Violent... 151
Corporations Strike Back... 152
The Union's New Friend - The Elected... 153
The C.I.O.. 153
Teamsters, Hoffa, and Robert Kennedy.. 155
U.S. Air Traffic Controller's Strike... 158
Are Unions Relevant Today?... 160
Labor Fraud... 166

Chapter 8 Worker Visas Take American Jobs....................... 173
Onshore vs. Offshore.. 173
Visa Alphabet Soup... 173
H-1B and White Collar Tech Workers.. 178
Other Companies Help Take American Jobs................................. 180
Trade Agreements Negotiated by Buffoons................................... 183
Canadian Nurses... 184
Cheaters in Small and Large Companies...................................... 192

Chapter 9 Offshoring: Bad for America................................. 197
History of Outsourcing... 197
Corporate Globalization Takes Outsourcing Offshore................... 198
Once Manufacturing Bones Are Picked, Service is Next............... 205
American Companies - Poor Management...................................... 207
Colleges and Universities Should Step to the Plate...................... 210
Is Protectionism Good or Bad?... 216
The Humanitarian Corporate Citizen... 226
The People First... 231

Chapter 10 AWOL Again on Illegal Aliens............................ 237
Social Security for Illegal Aliens Why Not?................................... 237
Does Illegal mean Illegal?... 238
Many Come Across; Few Go Back.. 241

Anchor Babies: The Term for the Children of Illegal Aliens.................... 247
How Much Does It Cost Taxpayers?... 260
The North American Union... 269
View From the U.S. Side of the Rio Grande....................................... 284
Do We Want Mexifornia... 287
Immigration and Nationality Act.. 306

Chapter 11 Theft-Proofing Election Process 309
Honest and Fair Elections?.. 311
Conspiracy?... 312
They Got Away With What?.. 314
Loopholes, Lawyers, & Judges 319
The Voting Machines Cheat?.. 324
Trust Us!.. 326
HAVA Not Optional.. 331
The Walgreen's Solution 339
Nothing Done By Computers Is Perfect 342
The More Eyes the Better.. 349

Part III A Few Silver Bullets! 355

Chapter12 General Solutions- Future of U. S. 355
Big Problems Bring Big Solutions.. 355
Representation, Democracy & Honorable Congressman 357
Is Anybody Listening? 358

Chapter 13 Silver Bullet forTaxes, More Taxes 371
Taxation by Confession 371
The IRS Administers the Problem 372
The Flat and the Fair Tax 374
What is the Fair Tax plan?... 374
What is the Flat Tax Plan: 375

Chapter 14 Silver Bullets for Corporations, Unions, Visas, and Offshoring 379
Fight for Liberty & Representation & U.S. Government 379
Corporate Power, Greed, & Corruption Solutions 380
The Reason for Republican Demonization of Trial Lawyers 385
Teddy the TrustBuster... 390
Countervailing Power - Labor Unions... 391
Labor Arbitrage --- Offshoring & H-1 B Visas 392
People v. Corporation... 397
Microsoft Jobs Going to India.. 403
AOL and Apple Heading to India... 404
The Simple Solution 408

Chapter 15 Silver Bullets : Illegal Aliens 413
Whether You Build It or Not, They Will Come!............................. 413
Pennsylvania is Not a Border State... 415
The Mexican Government 416
The Bush Border Legacy.. 419
U.S. Hypocrisy Re: illegal Aliens 424
Follow the Money.. 426
Amnesty for Illegals - Yes!... 427
Mexico Needs to Pay for its Own Poor.. 427
Block the borders, etc.. 436
Think About It Rationally:... 442

Appendices:
A The Declaration of Rights and Grievances 449
B The Articles of Association 455
C The Declaration of Independence..................................... 461
D The Articles of Confederation 467
E The Constitution of the U.S.A.. 477
F The Bill of Rights & Amendments..................................... 491
G Amendments Not Ratified 505
H Essays from Thomas Dawson 509
Illegal Aliens and Immigration... 511
All Immigration Problems Solved... 516
Labor Arbitrage? Better Known as Cheap Labor
Coin of the Realm 523

Preface Sample

Preface:

Americans today are overtaxed and just as in 1776, there is no visible representation. The spirit and reality of representative government that enlivened this country following the American Revolution has all but eroded into what we see today: an ad hoc litany of superficial homage to the discarded bedrock of what was once the very foundation of this great country.

Brian Kelly wrote this book because our representatives in the House, the Senate, in state legislatures and city councils have forgotten their duties as representatives of the people. Additionally, the president, the governors, the mayors, and other prefects of the people in the executive branches of governments across the land have conveniently forgotten that the primary fundamentals of our representative constitutional democracy start with representation. No single branch of government can claim immunity in the sale and resale of the United States to outside interests and American corporations. Each knows no moral bound or impediment to the gluttonous drive to perpetuate its self-serving two-party system. Even the judiciary is more caught up in preserving the two-party system than permitting deserving independents their opportunity to run for public office.

All of the candidates running for president in 2008 called for big changes. They were all right. They struck a chord with the American people on "change" but none offered specifics. Barack Obama came from no-place to be the cheerleader in charge. If we could have put a little substance on this plate, maybe we would have had a standard bearer. Right now, as sad as it may sound, it looks like we are headed down the same road for another four years. The final two Democrats and one of the Republicans has already been a representative, and Kelly wrote this book because it was representation that was not happening. Sending them back and rewarding them with a better position is probably not the right thing for the republic to do.

Obviously, from the 2008 primaries, there are few Americans who have tuned into this desperate need for change. We've had eight years of an unresponsive presidency with unprotected borders. Our Congress is fraught

Sample About the Author

Brian Kelly retired as an Assistant Professor in the Business Information Technology (BIT) Program at Marywood University, where he also served as the IBM i and Midrange Systems Technical Advisor to the IT Faculty. Kelly designed, developed, and taught many college and professional courses. He continues as a contributing technical editor to a number of technical industry magazines, including "The Four Hundred" and "Four Hundred Guru," published by IT Jungle. Kelly often has written for blogs such as Conservative Action Alerts.

Kelly is a former IBM Senior Systems Engineer. His specialty was problem solving for customers as well as implementing advanced operating systems and software on his client's machines. Brian is the author of 144 books and hundreds of magazine articles. Over half of his books and articles are about patriotic topics. Brian has been a frequent speaker at conferences throughout the United States.

Kelly was a candidate for the US Congress from Pennsylvania in 2010 and he ran for Mayor in his home town in 2015. He loves America but has no love for corrupt officials.

Checking out the Main Book Part of the Sample Pages

The above pages wrapped up the front matter section of the sample book front matter. The next page pictures are from the main book so you can get an idea of how the Chapter Head and the headings work together

Note when Chapter 1 begins that the page # restarts at 1 and the Roman Numeral formatting changes to English.

I show two pages of Chapter 1 and then I show the transition to Chapter 2 as an odd numbered page. Note that this sample book from the TOC is big, and because it is so big, I broke it down to parts 1, 2, and 3.

You can see how I dealt with the notion of Parts for this book. I put them on top of the Chapter designations. There have been books that I have written that I chose to put the Book Part changes on completely separate pages with blank pages in between. It is a matter of style. As the author, your style always wins unless your editor overrides you and you agree.

The headings for this book (not the sample book) are on the top of each page while the headings from the sample book are in the captured page pictures.

The last sample page that I show several pages from now is from the sample book's appendices. It is Appendix H just to show you how big this book actually is. Go ahead take a run through all the samples now.

Part I: The Problem

Chapter 1

We Get the Government We Deserve

America Is a Representative Democracy?

When the following thought marched into my mind only a few short months ago, "America is a representative democracy," I began to ask myself, isn't it time that we actually had some real "representation" from our so-called representative government? The way it now works provides far too much separation between us, the electors, and them, the elected officials coordinating our pooled resources for the alleged benefit of "everyone." But who is everyone? A genuinely compelling concern for our government or Disney-like utopian myth?

I propose the latter. Our government is wholly unaccountable. Even worse, its members, allegedly our civil servants, do not even seem to care for our own wellbeing. While running for office, it seems that incumbent and aspiring prospective officials saturate our consciousness day-in and day-out, wheedling us into their self-perpetuating power games with promises of responsiveness, unity, and even candor. Yet, even then, only one primary concern lurks on their minds, that *sine qua non* of their very daily existence, the next election.

2 Taxation Without Representation

A forthcoming election could be as distant as two years and still your
impending loss of job, perhaps due to a plant relocating to China, is
at best a secondary afterthought to the very men and women
promising you change, when you want it, and stability, again when
they believe you want it. Unfortunately, their priorities are one
dimensional and your job going to China isn't the focus. Eventually
they get re-elected and go off to Washington for yet another term.
The cycle starts again with the eternal candidate alternating between
Washington and their well insulated, gated communities far enough
from the common people that they don't have to care what you think.

It's Never Them

When they are about to raise your taxes, they are particularly
inconspicuous.   Being numbed to the excesses and decadent
corruption of everyday politics, you may not expect communication
and straight answers and so you are not disappointed. You hear
about the tax issues on TV or in the paper, not from your elected
because your opinion on the matter really doesn't matter. They
would rather converse via cellular or Blackberry with some of the only
entities who truly can garner their attention, co-Congressmen, the
affluent, and of course, major campaign donors. Discussing an
important issue with you, while seeming like a charming noble way
for a representative to spend an afternoon, is discarded as wanton.
It's dismissed simply because it would not tangibly benefit anyone's
reelection campaign which, as we have all learned, begins the day
oaths of office are sworn.

They want us to think that any tax increase is caused by imaginary
rival agents or economic forces beyond their control. They will
convey this to us with the sole purpose of acquiring our hard earned
money. Apparently, they promise, any burdens will fall on some
imaginary "other person" and we will remain unscathed. Horrifically
but as expected though, when we get our tax bills from the
bureaucracy, we find out that we were that "other" person. Since the
bureaucracy sent us the bill, we blame the bureaucracy, and again let

---

Chapter 2 Too Many Honorables

The Issues of Today

Something happened to representative government from the time of the Declaration of Independence and Constitution to the present. Though our constitutional democracy has survived for about 230 years, it is not at its healthiest right now. Here are just a few of the major problems that we are facing as a nation:

- The War on terrorism
- Wars in Iraq and Afghanistan
- L-1A and L-1B Foreign National Visas
- H-1B and D-1 Foreign National Visas
- Illegal immigration
- Excessive legal immigration
- Corporate power and greed
- Labor arbitrage / Offshoring
- Jobs
- Election Process Corruption
- Healthcare availability and affordability
- Institution of marriage
- Respect for life
- Influence of Special Interests
- Lobbying
- Private Property Confiscation
- Political and Corporate Corruption
- Energy and Oil
- Homeland Security
- Social Security
- Free Trade

Appendices (Appendix H)

Appendix H

Essays of Thomas Dawson

Surprise in Email

While I was researching this book, I came across numerous anecdotes, many of which were nothing short of amazing and phenomenally insightful. One thing I have learned in my 60 years (my 60th Birthday party was just last Friday) is that nobody knows it all and as a corollary, there is something brilliant that is ready to be discovered every day. I was so impressed with the writings of Thomas Dawson, both in content and style that I wrote him a month ago and asked if I could use his material in this book. At the time, I had intended to use some excerpts of his works in the main body of some of the chapters in which his insights applied. But, when I received Tom's note yesterday, I had already finished the book and was in final editing.

I thought about an insertion here or there and then I decided that, since Mr. Dawson offered no strings on his granting permission for his works, I would print them as his essays for your reading pleasure and give him the full credit he deserves. This was his note to me. I have never met him but you can feel the goodness of this gentleman in his words:

Mr Kelly:

Sorry I couldn't get back to you sooner. You are more than welcome to use any of my material at your discretion, either in

· Index¶

¶...Section Break (Continuous)...

1890 Sherman Antitrust, 390¶
2008 Primaries, 381¶
Aaron Sargent, 250¶
Acapulco, 435¶
Accreditation, 210¶
Afghanistan, 19¶
AFL, 150, 151, 152, 153, 154, 155, 170, 276¶
AFSCME, 154, 171¶
AIG, 184¶
Air Traffic Controller, 158, 159¶
Alcoholic Beverage tax, 59¶
Aldous Huxley, 11¶
Almon Leroy Way, 45¶
Ambassador, 36¶
Amendments, Constitution107, 109, 110, 247, 248, 363, 480, 487, 491, 494, 505¶
American dream, 117, 182, 183, 244, 302, 393¶
American Government, 45, 356, 379¶
American History, 104, 139, 254¶
American Indians, 84, 85, 86¶
American Jobs, 164, 173, 180, 218, 398¶
American Patriots, 91¶
Amnesty, 254, 268, 274, 275, 276, 427, 512¶
Amusement Tax, 60, 64¶
Anchor Babies, 247¶
Apple, 404¶
Argentina, 428¶
Arthur Anderson, 123, 124, 125, 127, 223, 398¶
Articles of Association, 88, 102, 455¶
Articles of Confederation, 8, 96, 99, 100, 103, 104, 105, 106, 380, 467, 473¶
Assembly, 78, 85, 323¶
Automatic Citizenship, 254¶
Bangladesh, 139, 392¶
Barbara Stanwyck, 360¶
Battles, 91, 92, 93, 99, 104, 379¶
Beer Taxes, 61¶
Benign Oligarchy, 8¶

399, 400, 401, 403, 404, 405, 406, 408, 436¶
Bill of Rights, 50, 107, 109, 139, 491, 492, 494, 505¶
Bill O'Reilly, 264, 386, 426¶
Bi-Partisanship, 276¶
Blackberry, 2, 348¶
Bob Fitrakis, 325, 352¶
Bob Ney, 40¶
Bobby Amory, 156¶
Border Patrol, 245, 246, 304, 417¶
Boston Harbor, 86, 87¶
Boston Tea Party, 87, 88¶
Boston to Concord, 91¶
British Army, 84¶
British East India Company, 136, 138, 139¶
British Goods, 89¶
British Parliament, 86, 449, 450¶
Broken Government, 4¶
Bush, 14, 40, 53, 121, 179, 182, 183, 185, 190, 204, 218, 239, 242, 244, 246, 268, 269, 270, 274, 278, 279, 280, 281, 285, 344, 351, 373, 377, 385, 386, 413, 419, 420, 425, 426¶
Buy Mexico, 434, 435¶
C.I.O., 153, 154, 276¶
Cabot, 73, 74¶
Campaign Donors, 2¶
Careerism, 14¶
Carl Romanelli, 311, 312, 315, 316, 317, 322, 353¶
Carly Fiorina, 223, 224, 227, 229¶
Carpenters Hall, 88¶
Catholic, 10, 298, 452¶
Caucasian, 303¶
Central Pacific, 132¶
Charity Gaming Tax, 59¶
Charles Crocker, 133¶
Charter form, 75¶
Checks and balances, 8, 9, 50, 112, 358¶
China, 2, 6, 14, 139, 182, 201, 202, 209, 210, 215, 216, 222, 226, 249, 274, 291, 392, 396, 520, 521¶

Cigarette Tax, 59, 61, 64¶
Cities & Municipalities Tax, 61¶
Citizen Corporation, 387¶
Citizenship Reform Act, 252¶
Civics Lesson, 44, 69¶
Clarence, 361¶
Clinton, 14, 40, 63, 97, 159, 182, 183, 185, 208, 255, 257, 272, 386, 420, 435¶
COBOL, 530¶
Cognizant, 195¶
Coin of the Realm, 16, 523, 529¶
Colleges, 210, 213, 234¶
Collis Huntington,, 133¶
Colonial Currency, 111¶
Colonial Suffrage, 79¶
Colonialism, 80¶
Columbus, 73, 74, 75¶
Concord Hymn, 91¶
Congressional representatives, 20, 153¶
Congressmen, 2, 43, 182, 358¶
Constitution, 6, 7, 8, 9, 15, 17, 19, 24, 37, 38, 48, 49, 50, 51, 52, 53, 98, 99, 101, 103, 104, 105, 106, 107, 108, 109, 111, 112, 113, 117, 125, 130, 131, 139, 140, 170, 247, 248, 250, 252, 253, 270, 285, 317, 325, 362, 363, 364, 365, 367, 380, 387, 388, 419, 450, 477, 482, 484, 485, 487, 488, 491, 492, 494, 495, 496, 497, 498, 499, 500, 501, 502, 503, 505, 506, 507, 508¶
Constitutional democracy, 8, 19, 44, 46, 47, 48, 101, 105, 106, 112¶
Constitutionalism, 47, 51¶
Continental Association, 88¶
Copper, 428¶

¶... Section Break (Even Page)...

¶

LETS·GO·PUBLISH!·Books: ¶

Sold at www.itjungle.com, www.mcpressonline.com, www.bookhawkers.com. ¶
LETS GO PUBLISH! www.letsgopublish.com Our titles include the following: email info@ letsgopublish.com for ordering information¶

¶

The System i5 Pocket Developers' Guide.¶
Comprehensive Pocket Guide to all of the AS/400 and System i5 development tools - DFU, SDA, etc. "SDA", etc. You'll also get a big bonus with chapters on Architecture, Work Management, and Subfile Coding. ¶

The System i5 Pocket Database Guide.¶
Complete Pocket Guide to System i5 integrated relational database (DB2/400) - physical and logical files and DB operations - Union, Projection, Join, etc. Written in a part tutorial and part reference style, this book has tons of DDS coding samples, from the simple to the sublime. ¶

The System i5 Pocket SQL Guide.¶
Complete Pocket Guide to SQL as implemented on System i5. A must have for SQL developers new to System i5. It is very compact yet very comprehensive and it is example driven. Written in a part tutorial and part reference style, this book has tons of SQL coding samples, from the simple to the sublime. ¶

The System i5 Pocket Query Guide. ¶
If you have been spending money for years educating your Query users, and you find you are still spending, or you've given up, this book is right for you. This one QuikCourse covers all Query options.¶

The System i Pocket RPG & RPG IV Guide. ¶
Comprehensive RPG & RPGIV Textbook -- Over 900 pages Published in 2006. This is the one RPG book to have if you are not having more than one. All areas of the language covered smartly in a convenient sized book. ¶

The System i RPG Tutorial and Lab Guide. ¶
Your guide to a hands-on Lab experience. Contains CD with Lab exercises and PowerPoint's. Great companion to the above textbook or can be used as a standalone for student Labs or tutorial purposes.¶

The WebFacing/exe."WebFacing"] Application Design & Development Guide: ¶
The Step by Step Guide to designing green screen System i5 applications intended to be deployed on the Web./exe."RPG"][exe."COBOL"] ·¶

The System i5 Express Web Implementer's Guide. Your one stop guide to ordering, installing, fixing, configuring, and using WebSphere Express, Apache, WebFacing, System i5 Access for Web, and HATS/LE.¶

Can the AS/400 Survive IBM[XE."IBM".]?¶
Exciting book about the AS/400 in an System i5 World.¶

The All-Everything Machine¶
The story about IBM[XE."IBM".]'s finest computer server.¶

Chip Wars¶
The story of the ongoing war between Intel and AMD and the upcoming was between Intel and IBM[XE."IBM".]. This book may cause you to buy or sell somebody's stock. ·¶
¶

END of SAMPLES

Chapter 6 Final Preparations for Publishing

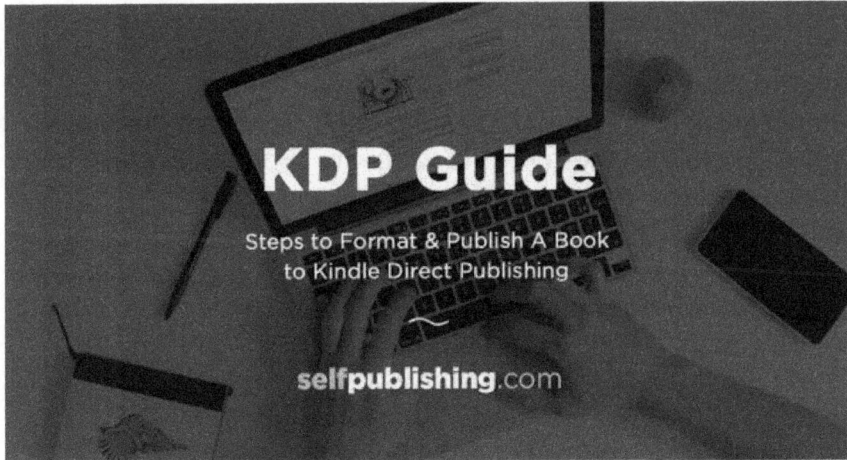

This is an important step

When you get to this point in the preparation of your book for publishing, you will have already written the front matter as well as the main part of your manuscript and you will have edited it at least three times. You will have edited it and you will have assured that it is structured into proper sized chapters organized into Word book sections. At this point, you now believe that all other things being equal, your book in this manuscript form is ready to be published.

Even though you are brimming with confidence, there are still more things to assure and to verify before you can take your book and upload it to Amazon KDP or any other publishing house.

You may find some of the additional to-do's that we outline unnecessary for this your first publishing venture but it is good to think about them as they may be valuable and easier than you think to implement. Here are the steps and sub steps that you should examine as your final checklist before beginning the publishing process. When you need to complete a step in this list, move the task name to your active to-do list so that you can accomplish it before you begin the publishing phase for your project.

1. Select trim size
2. Make sure your table of contents has been generated properly
3. Visually scan book manuscript to see if additional images are needed.
4. Visually scan book manuscript assuring headings are not orphans and that there are no widow or orphans in your paragraphs.
5. Determine cover design
6. Assemble your front matter
7. Determine whether you want to create an Imprint. Consider something catchy such as Lets Go Publish! And consider creating a logo for this book and those to come.
8. Build a web site for your Imprint or for yourself
9. Decide whether you want to sell books
10. Apply for copyright and file library of congress paperwork
11. Make a decision on whether to use your own ISBN

Select trim size.

The trim size is your books' size. My recommendation for your first book is to set the size at 6" X 9" This is a standard for many publishers and it works very well with Amazon KDP.

It is essential that your word document book size matches the trim size selected in CreateSpace. For example, if you want a 5.5 X 8.5 book, your word margins cannot be set at 8.5 X 11. So, if you have not yet changed your margins in word, set them before you do anything else. Then, check the effect on your pagination from changing the trim size. You will more than likely find issues with orphan and widow headings as well as orphans and widows in paragraphs. Page through your entire manuscript before you go to the next step. Now is the time to get this done before you move to your next step.

Getting your word document ready for upload

With my other printers, I did not get grammar advice even from an automaton. My books were always done well but often in the gutter of the book (between the pages), it was difficult to see all the text as there was just enough white space but little more to make the book easy to handle and easy to read without opening the book wider to see what was in the "book's gutter." Amazon's KDP offers the opportunity to gain great knowledge about such things.

Use one word doc text-page per PDF-page; One PDF-page per page number. Your document's dimensions will be the book's final trim size, plus bleed (optional) with margins. If you don't understand bleed, feel free to look it up on the Internet but for your first book, do not select bleed. That is very important to know. Here are some facts that will help in preparing a perfectly well-written and well-structured manuscript for publishing. It helps to get familiar with all of these terms when you are self-publishing.

Trim Size
This is the final cut-size of your book in width by height.
Learn more about choosing a trim size from the Amazon KDP site.

Margins
Check out this chart that shows the gutter spacing and the margins for various page counts. If your manuscript prepared by Word does not measure up, then before you submit to CreateSpace, you must correct the issue in the document with Word.

Page Count	Inside Margin	Outside Margins
24 to 150 pages	**.375"**	at least .25"
151 to 300 pages	**.5"**	at least .25"
301 to 500 pages	**.625"**	at least .25"
501 to 700	**.75"**	at least .25"

Page Count	Inside Margin	Outside Margins
pages		
701 to 828 pages	**.875"**	at least .25"

Gutter margins are by the book's binding. You'll want a wider margin for longer (thicker) books. See the table above for what to set your inside margins to.

Outside margins are the page edges opposite of the binding, and the top and bottom margins. All live text and images must have an outside margin of at least .25" – Amazon KDP recommends an outside margin of at least .5"

These are the margin settings for the book you are reading. The numbers are formatted through the custom margin's settings drop down from the Page Layout Tab in Word.

Page Setup   ?   ✕

| Margins | Paper | Layout |

Margins

Top:	0.4"		Bottom:	0.5"	
Inside:	0.5"		Outside:	0.4"	
Gutter:	0"		Gutter position:	Left	

Orientation

 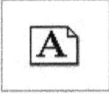

Portrait   Landscape

Pages

Multiple pages: Mirror margins

Preview

 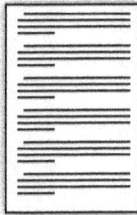

Apply to: Whole document

| Set As Default | | OK | Cancel |

Make sure your table of contents has been generated properly

Whenever you change margins in a book, it is good to scan the entire book to be sure that your change did not produce results that you would not like. Sometimes for example a picture caption gets separated from the picture or a widow or orphan appears that needs to be addressed. Take nothing for granted. Word is good at helping with a lot of stuff but it is not perfect.

When your book is as you want it go to the page in the front matter where you want the table of contents created. Choose reference or insert/reference and then create your table of contents.

If you choose to have an index and you have marked all the test you want for entries, go ahead and position yourself to the back of the book where you want the index and create it using word's auto create function.

Scrutinize your generated table of contents and your generated index. If they are not as expected, you must correct them inside your document and recreate the TOC and the Index.

See if additional images are needed.

Every author knows what they want and do not want. If you have all the images you think you need or want in your book, then mark this task complete. Otherwise, scan your manuscript for insertion points for images, find those images on your PC, in your email attachments on the Internet or in artist sites. If the images require payment, make sure you pay for them before including them in your new book. Sometimes all you need to do is write the image owner and they will send you an email with the necessary permission. There is work involved for images. Sorry!

Assure that headings are not orphans.

An orphan is a paragraph-opening line that appears by itself at the bottom of a page or column, thus separated from the rest of the text. This area may in fact be a heading at any level while the paragraph text is on the next page. One reading a book with orphans and widows blames the author for such distractions.

As you know, Word creates new pages automatically as you enter text. You don't have to do a thing, but you can exercise control when you don't like the results. One situation that might arise as noted above is keeping a heading with the following paragraph. Sometimes that type of break won't matter. When it does, you can force Word to keep the heading with its text. You do this In the Pagination section, just check the Keep Lines Together option and Word will make sure that the potential orphan stays with the paragraph.

Don't trust Word to do your job. When you finish your book and are ready to submit it for printing, scan the pages and look at the top and bottom of each page for ugly, unsightly stray text. Then, remove it. When you create your PDF for submission, read the pdf version to make sure it mirrors the word version.

Determine your cover design

Before you do anything make sure that you review Chapter 4. I have the pleasure of using Michele Thomas for special cover designs and she is very, very, good. When you go to amazon.com/author/brianwkelly, you will see the great covers which she has designed. She is from Wilkes-Barre, PA and she can be reached through the phone book. You can most often tell the books that I designed using the KDP Cover Creator, a phenomenal tool from the ones Michele designed.

If you cannot afford a professional cover design for your book, study some other covers for books such as yours and then plan to use the KDP Cover Designer to create a cover that is acceptable.

Build your front matter.

Front matter is something that is foreign to most readers and new writers. It will help for you to review Chapters 3 & 5 which should be helpful in composing your front matter. Look at the front matter in this book and see if you would like something like it.

Determine whether you want to create an Imprint

You may also want to hire a designer to create a logo for your imprint, whether it is a company name or your own name. It looks good on a book. An imprint of a publisher is a trade name under which a work is published. A single publishing company may have multiple imprints, with the different imprints often used by the publisher to market works to different demographic consumer segments. When you print using print on demand services such as Amazon KDP, you are the publisher if you choose. For years, I have used the imprint Lets Go Publish! as originally, I intended to offer services to help others publish.

Build a web site for your Imprint or for yourself

You may or may not want to do this but if you have the time and you plan to write more books than this first one, it is a good idea. You can also set up a Facebook page for your imprint, yourself, and/or your new book.

Let's suppose you either have an imprint or you want to use your name and your writing collaborator's if you have one as a web site name. Suppose you are Mary and your partner in this project is Joe. You might want to go to Godaddy.com and see if maryjoebooks is available After you type maryjoebooks.com, if you did it today, you would see a page like that shown on the next page:

If you are pleased, you can buy the name for about $10.00. Once you have the name, you need a web site to host the information which you want to show on the Internet's World Wide Web. Web Hosting is what makes your site visible on the web.

GoDaddy and many other providers of Internet Service offer fast, reliable plans for every need - from a basic blog to a high-powered site.

From the GoDaddy panel on this page, you would click on the Hosting tab and then select web hosting. From there, you could pick a hosting plan that fits your needs. The Economy Plan at $3.99 per month (ten years ago) is more than likely all you need. It also includes a free domain name so you would not have to buy maryjoebooks.com if you pick this option.

Once you get your website and domain attached to your web site, you can use a tool such as WordPress or Joomla or others to build your site. GoDaddy and other service companies provide a lot of information about how to get this done. There are a lot of techno-geeks that you may know who would do this for you for a small fee.

Decide whether you want to sell books

If you want to sell your own books and maybe some T-shirts and other doo-dads on your own site. GoDaddy and other Internet service providers offer plans to help you engage the Internet. To see the plans, from the GoDaddy panel on the other page, click on all-products and then online store. It takes some thinking and some work to set up an online store.

Whether you choose to sell your books or not, Amazon KDP has arrangements through Amazon and Kindle and many other booksellers to get your book sold on the Internet.

Apply for Copyright and file library of congress paperwork

Whether you apply or not, your book is automatically copyrighted to you because you wrote it. You may choose to give this up to a publisher but my experience in recent years is that authors are demanding to hold the copyright.

To register the fact that you wrote a book or other creative work that you want copyrighted, simply go to copyright.gov, the website set up by the Library of Congress. There is an online portal to register copyrights for photographs, sculptures and written works. Fill out the form, pay the fee and you are registered.

Make a decision on whether to use your own ISBN

Most publishers, even self-publishers, especially those who were out there before Amazon KDP buy ten or perhaps 100 ISBN numbers at a time from Bowker Services and then assign them to their next ten or 100 books. If you take a book that you have written and load it to Amazon KDP, you may use the same ISBN as the original for the book under your publishing imprint.

An ISBN is an International Standard Book Number. ISBNs were 10 digits in length up to the end of December 2006, but since 1 January 2007 they now always consist of 13 digits. ISBNs are calculated using a specific mathematical formula and include a check digit to validate the number. No bookseller will sell a book without an ISBN so they are very important

If you want to buy one ISBN or ten or x, here is what you do. Go to myidentifiers.com, the ISBN website run by Bowker, which is the only company authorized to administer the ISBN program in the United States. Click on "ISBN Identifiers" and you'll be taken to a page where you can buy 1, 10, 100 or 1000 ISBNs. Sometimes they have sales where you cans save 5% or 10%.

Why does this matter? Amazon KDP will provide you with a free ISBN but you lose certain rights. Discussions on the user's groups are not definitive but this post gives a good perspective: This is from somebody other than me:

"I posed this exact question with Amazon KDP yesterday. This is the answer: When you use an ISBN number from KDP then you are not the publisher, KDP is and they will have rights to your book. However, if you purchase your own ISBN number (from Bowker, for example,) then you will be the publisher and owner with the rights to do whatever you want to with YOUR book (publisher-wise)"

When you first begin the publishing process with CreateSpace, one of the first questions they ask is if you will use your imprint and one of the next is whether you will use their ISBN or your own. Make sure you know what your decision is on whose ISBN you will use.

Chapter 7 Using Amazon KDP for Publishing

Amazon KDP loves all authors

Amazon KDP takes pride in saying that "Authors are at the heart of what we do." I taught marketing at the collegiate level and so I know how to detect BS from reality. The proof is in the action not the words. Amazon KDP backs up their promises with reality.

It really is that simple. The Company's innovative free tools and top-notch professional services make both publishing and distribution easier than ever. Most new authors want to have a nice hard copy book in their hands representing their hard work. It is a prize unto itself and typically well-deserved.

The next moment however is lonely unless you are using Amazon KDP. The service not only publishes your book very efficiently and mostly cost-free, the company also distributes your book at your choosing at no additional cost all around the world.

And, so it pays to self-publish with Amazon KDP. The royalty structure is better than the big publishing houses, especially for a new guy.

I can attest to that having lived in both worlds. It is great for a company to be able to make money and give you a great share of the profits. Amazon KDP uses industry-leading economics and this means putting more in your pocket.

I still cannot understand how they get it done and why they are not asking me for some contributions. Can you believe that the book manufacturing (printing etc.) and shipping is all taken care of.

Amazon KDP keeps your book in-stock, without inventory How do they do that. They print it on demand immediately when an order comes in. It really is amazing. Books are made on-demand when customers order.

When I used Offset Paperback (OPM), even if I was not sure I could sell a book, I had to order several hundred dollar's worth of books to get one printed.

Amazon KDP will print as little as one proof or as many as five and when you say go, they make your book for sale across the world.

There is a large array of no-charge options, including a free Interior Reviewer and Cover Creator. Together Amazon's KDP is like no other company in the business. It can create the book that you have always wanted.

Chapter 8 Getting Started with Kindle Direct Publishing KDP

A Service of Amazon

The mechanics of signing up are quite simple

Follow the next several pages by clicking and typing as requested:

https://kdp.amazon.com/en_US/help/topic/G200620010
Click above.
V

Create a KDP Account ✕ +

← → C 🔒 kdp.amazon.com/en_US/help/topic/G200620010

ect
lishing   Bookshelf | Reports | Community | KDP Select

Q Topic or Keyword

Accounts > Create a KDP Account

Create a KDP Account

Already have an Amazon account? Sign in to Kindle Direct Publishing (KDP) with your existing Amazon username and password.

kdp jumpstart
A guide to publishing on Amazon

Don't have an Amazon account? Go to KDP and click **Sign up**. Then click **Create your KDP account** and enter your name, email address, and a secure password.

Once you've created your account, you'll need to enter author, payment, and tax information. Browse the topics below to learn more.

Author/publisher information

Getting paid

Click on KDP above unless you already have an Amazon account and want to use it.

amazon

Create account

Your name

Email

Password

At least 6 characters

i Passwords must be at least 6 characters.

Re-enter password

Create your Amazon account

By creating an account, you agree to Amazon's
Conditions of Use and Privacy Notice.

Already have an account? Sign-In ›

f

Fill in your information above and sign on.

amazon

Sign-In

Email (phone for mobile accounts)

buzz@buzz.net

Password   Forgot your password?

••••••••••••

Sign-In

By continuing, you agree to Amazon's Conditions of Use and Privacy Notice.

☐ Keep me signed in. Details ▾

New to Amazon?

Create your Amazon account

You are now ready to begin to use KDP

Just look at the form above. If people were not complaining about how hard it is to get a voter's card, I would cite getting a voter's card as an example of how easy it is to sign up and become active on KDP. They do not care if you drive or eat tomatoes or are vegan or you are a meat lover. They want all writers who want to be book authors to be part of their program. It is a great program by the way!

To become a KDP Author, even without ever having a book uploaded, just fill out the forms above and click on Create your Amazon Account.

If you are here in this dialogue, you have already done what you were supposed to.

Without you feeling even a bit queasy, your account will be created and you can then engage in publishing activities—no matter who you are or who you want to be. it is the best secret in publishing circles.

It helps to know that simply by signing up, along with your FREE Amazon Kindle Direct Publishing (KDP) "membership," you also get:

- ✓ Access to FREE online tools to help you publish faster and easier
- ✓ Free digital proofing to view your book's cover and interior online, anytime
- ✓ Wide distribution of your book in the U.S. and Europe
- ✓ Easy tools to help create a Kindle eBook at no extra cost
- ✓ Industry-leading royalty rates
- ✓ World-class member support 24/7
- ✓ And much more...

Now, of course, we have to get that book of yours published.

You may recall that in this book we discussed a two-file and a single-book file method for creating your electronic manuscript. For KDP, you must use your single file manuscript. If you have chosen KDP but originally used the two file approach, simply take the two files and merge them into one. You can use highlight, copy, and paste to get this merge done with no hassle. Then convert your .doc or .docx Word file to PDF and that is all you need to do before you upload your manuscript file.

I am the last one to suggest that you can send slop or garbage up to Amazon KDP or that they are so hard pressed that they will put their best people on the project and send you back a completed 100% perfect manuscript for approval. Don't even try it. Sorry that is not how it works. In fact, you are the most important person in the book publishing process with Amazon's KDP.

Therefore, for your mission to be successful, you need to learn all you can. Otherwise, manuscripts will be rejected by the auto-proofer even before you get to communicate with a KDP Agent.

In other words, KDP's print on demand requires stuff from the most important person in the process—the author, aka Y-O-U. They need simple information to start such as specific information about each title that will contribute to the overall success of your final product.

These requirements are necessary so KDP can provide you with a reliable and cost-effective service. Understanding and meeting these requirements will help make the process of setting up your title easier and more efficient. At this point in the process, you have not even submitted your manuscript but that part is coming.

Copy-editing

You can get by on the cheap if your manuscript is already well edited. But if it is not, there are a load of companies that you may choose to copy edit your work. You can also contract with a local English teacher which is what I did in the beginning. You can also choose to go it alone and take your best shot. If your book passes muster, you will get it published. If not Amazon KDP's automatic editing will tell you what is wrong.

A professional editor will use The Chicago Manual of Style, 17th edition, the preferred style guide in the book publishing industry, and the Merriam-Webster dictionary while editing your manuscript. Make sure that you are willing to pay for this and get a good feel for its cost before you proceed.

A professional editor will help you very positively if this is what you want. The editor will review your manuscript using the Microsoft Word Track Changes feature and provide a line edit that corrects typos and ensures consistency in Grammar, Punctuation, and Spelling. In addition, an editor will also provide an Editorial Letter explaining the suggested changes made in the manuscript. You ultimately make the changes.

Like I said, an English teacher down the block may be able to do the same but that is up to you. The good news is that without spending a million dollars, you can be reasonably assured that your book won't make your neighbors snicker.

Chapter 9 Creating Your First Book Title with Amazon KDP

To begin Type in KDP.AMAZON.COM

amazon

Sign-In

Email (phone for mobile accounts)

buzz@buzz.net

Password   Forgot your password?

•••••••••••

Sign-In

By continuing, you agree to Amazon's Conditions of Use and Privacy Notice.

☐ Keep me signed in. Details ▼

New to Amazon?

Create your Amazon account

Sign on and set up your first new title

Now that you have registered with KDP and you have your book manuscript ready to upload in PDF form, let's begin the process by signing on.

Type in kdp.amazon.com and press enter on your PC keyboard from your browser window. You will get a panel whose left side looks similar to the panel in Figure 9-1

Figure 9-1 Amazon KDP First Page After Sign-On

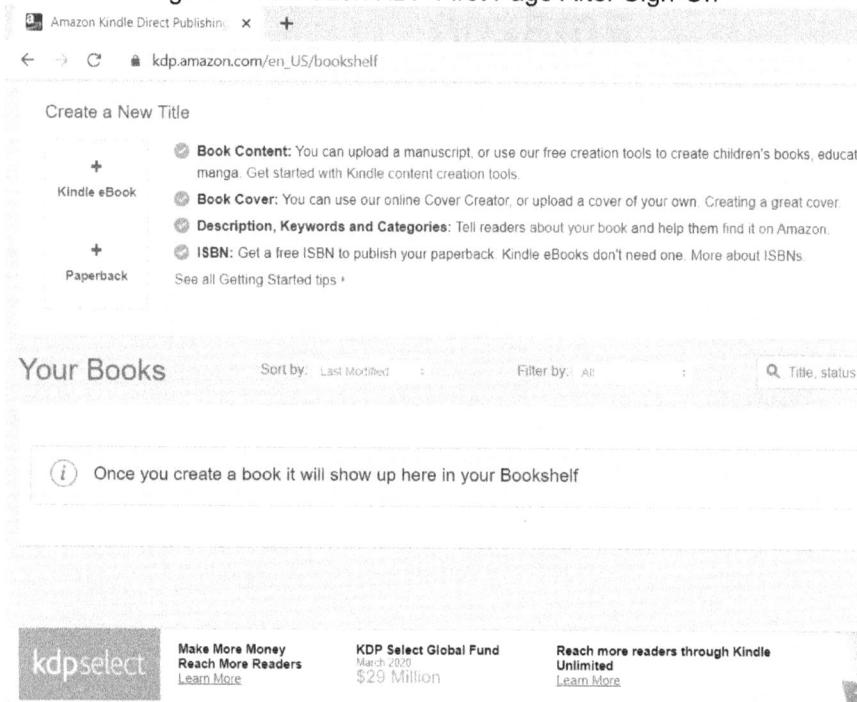

As you can see on the left side, there are two plus signs to create new documents. You can create a kindle eBook or you can create a paperback book. We will let you work through kindle on your own. For our lessons on getting a book self-published, we will create a hard copy book, which is also known as a paperback.

To begin, the process, you will click on the + Paperback option on the left side of the panel.

Figure 9-2 Add a New Title

Paperback Details
i In Progress...

Paperback Content
i Not Started...

Language

Choose your paperback's primary language (the language in whic

English   ⇕

Book Title

Enter your title as it appears on your book cover. Learn more abo

Book Title

My New Book

Subtitle (Optional)

It is a hum dinger

You can add information about your new title on this panel. Scroll down after you type in your title My New Book and the subtitle It is a hum dinger. It is good to have a subtitle most of the time. .

Aspiring authors often hesitate to get specific in their book's titles—there's a fear of turning readers off, or potentially spoiling plot points. At Lets Go Publish!, our advice is that your subtitle is the chance to tell potential readers exactly what your book is about. ... Your subtitle should be crystal clear.

Dave Chesson has an article out on the internet titled HOW TO SELECT A SUBTITLE THAT SELLS. It is worth a read before you select your sub title. The link is https://kindlepreneur.com/how-to-select-a-subtitle-that-sells/.
Dave suggests among other things that "Subtitles are where an author can hone in and pack a punch with an artful turn-of-phrase. The subtitle has a distinct role apart from the primary title. While your book title clearly tells readers what the book is about, the job of the multi-faceted

subtitle is to speak to the precise benefits readers will receive from your book."

In his article, he teaches you:

- Amazon requirements to selecting a subtitle
- Step-by-step to selecting a subtitle that sells
- Book subtitle examples

After you type in the subtitle, use the scroll bars to page down and fill in the rest of the stuff you need. Some blanks are optional.

You'll be asked if your book is part of a series, if it is a particular edition #, the name of the author (you), and any contributors you would like to formally recognize as being part of the effort. After sliding the scroll bar more, you'll then be asked about description, publishing rights, and keywords. You can see how I filled these in   below:

Figure 9-3 Type Description etc.

Description	This will appear on your book's Amazon detail page. Why do book descriptions matter? ▾
	we show you the ins and outs of writing a book using Microsoft Word as your author tool, w your book, create table of contents and indexes; how to format your chapters and lots more. upload your document file to CreateSpace so that you too can one day be a famous author.
Publishing Rights	● I own the copyright and I hold necessary publishing rights. What are publishing rights?
	○ This is a public domain work What is a public domain work? ▾
Keywords	Choose up to 7 keywords that describe your book. How do I choose keywords? ▾
	Your Keywords (Optional)
	"How to publish" "publishing"

Keywords are used for people to find your book on google searches.

Figure 9-4 Click on Choose categories and select the right one for your book

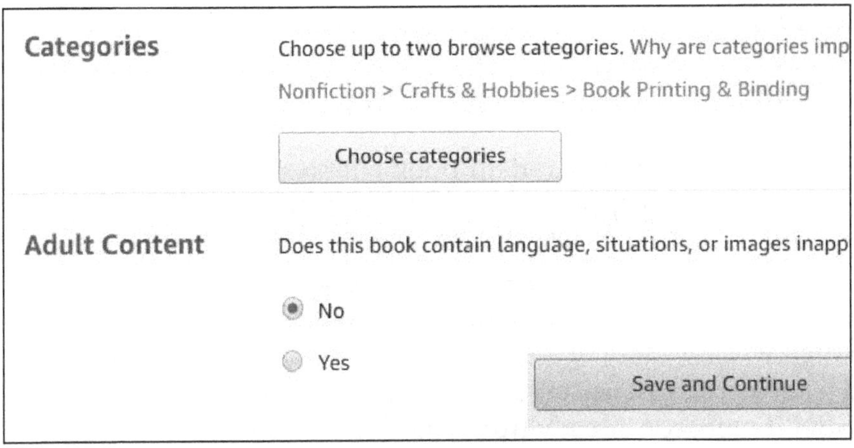

Categories	Choose up to two browse categories. Why are categories imp
	Nonfiction > Crafts & Hobbies > Book Printing & Binding
	Choose categories
Adult Content	Does this book contain language, situations, or images inapp
	⦿ No
	○ Yes
	Save and Continue

When finished with page1, click on Save & Continue

Figure 9-5 Enter ISBN, your Imprint & Date

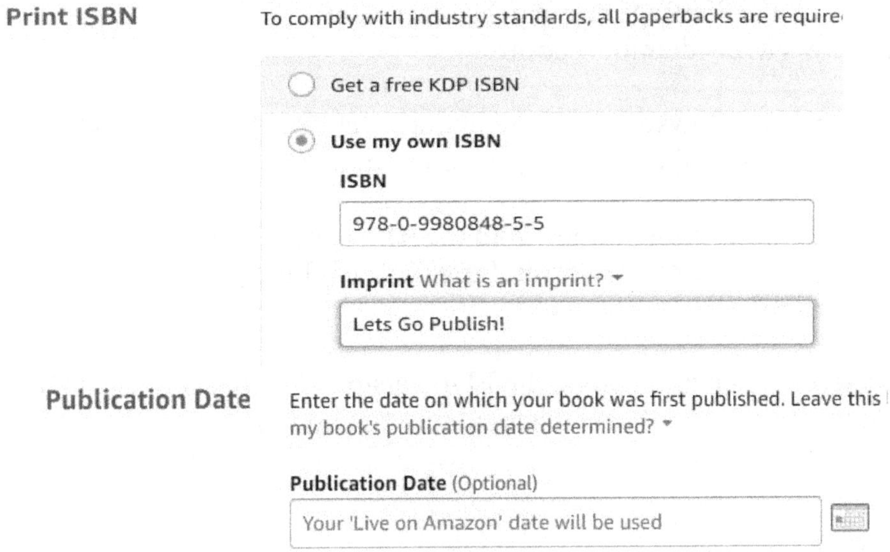

Print ISBN   To comply with industry standards, all paperbacks are require

○ Get a free KDP ISBN

⦿ **Use my own ISBN**

ISBN

978-0-9980848-5-5

Imprint What is an imprint? ▾

Lets Go Publish!

Publication Date   Enter the date on which your book was first published. Leave this
my book's publication date determined? ▾

Publication Date (Optional)

Your 'Live on Amazon' date will be used

Use the default as shown under Publication date.

The Print ISBN Question needs some explanation. For your first book, you might choose to use Amazon's free ISBN #. I am in the business so I buy my own ISBNs from a company called Bowker for about $500 for 100 ISBN numbers. One ISBN might cost as much as $100 so before you proceed to this question make sure you know what you are doing with ISBNs. If you plan to write a lot of books, buy at least ten ISBNs and you will own the rights to your books if they are successful in the marketplace.

More on ISBNs

An ISBN, or International Standard Book Number, is a unique 10-digit number assigned to every published book. An ISBN identifies a title's binding, edition, and publisher. An EAN, or European Article Number, is a 13-digit number assigned to every book to provide a unique identifier for international distributors. The 10-digit ISBN is converted to a 13-digit EAN by adding a 978 prefix and changing the last digit. To publish a book, you can use either a free KDP ISBN or use your own valid ISBN (purchased directly from your ISBN agency).

Amazon tells you more about ISBNs at this URL:
https://kdp.amazon.com/en_US/help/topic/G201834170

Bowker, the ISBN Registrar can be reached at
https://www.myidentifiers.com/.

Unfortunately, Bowker may be temporarily closed with COVID-19 precautions so try them before you count on them in the near future.

Next select your print options from the next page option. Make sure you recall the trim size of your book. I use 6" X 9". I use glossy and black & white printing.

Next scroll down and upload the PDF version of your manuscript. By clicking on the upload paperback manuscript button.
Figure 9-6 Upload your book & cover files or use the Cover Creator

Manuscript	Upload a manuscript of your book interior content. For best results, paperback. You can also upload a DOC (.doc), DOCX (.docx), HTML (PDF manuscripts. Learn more about manuscripts or download a KD
	Upload paperback manuscript

Book Cover	We recommend a book cover for a good reader experience. You can book cover. Learn more about book covers or download a KDP temp

⊙ **Use Cover Creator to make your book cover (upload your** (

Launch Cover Creator

No Cover Uploaded

○ Upload a cover you already have (print-ready PDF only)

After you click on the upload button, it asks you to locate your pdf manuscript on your PC. Click on it or it and click on upload or open.

Figure 9-7 Pick your file to upload

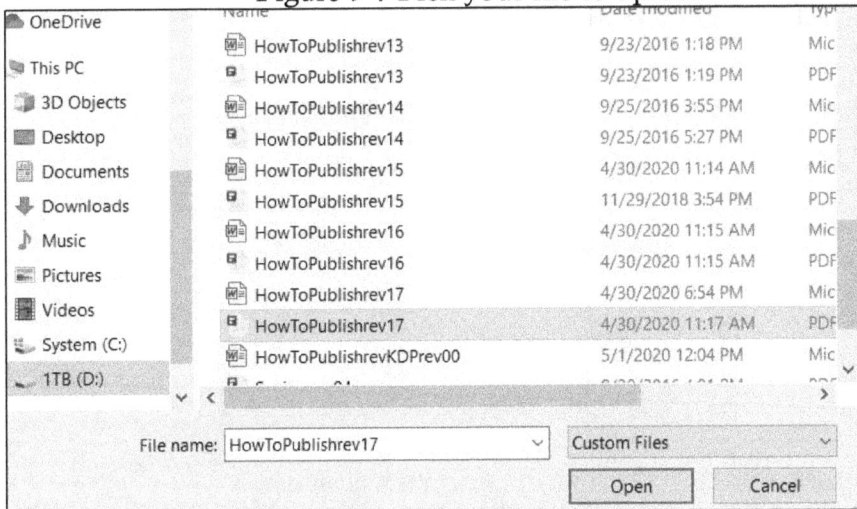

	Name	Date modified	Typ
OneDrive			
This PC	HowToPublishrev13	9/23/2016 1:18 PM	Mic
3D Objects	HowToPublishrev13	9/23/2016 1:19 PM	PDF
Desktop	HowToPublishrev14	9/25/2016 3:55 PM	Mic
Documents	HowToPublishrev14	9/25/2016 5:27 PM	PDF
Downloads	HowToPublishrev15	4/30/2020 11:14 AM	Mic
Music	HowToPublishrev15	11/29/2018 3:54 PM	PDF
Pictures	HowToPublishrev16	4/30/2020 11:15 AM	Mic
Videos	HowToPublishrev16	4/30/2020 11:15 AM	PDF
System (C:)	HowToPublishrev17	4/30/2020 6:54 PM	Mic
1TB (D:)	HowToPublishrev17	4/30/2020 11:17 AM	PDF
	HowToPublishrevKDPrev00	5/1/2020 12:04 PM	Mic

File name: HowToPublishrev17   Custom Files

Open   Cancel

Pick the manuscript to upload

Complete the upload process and launch the cover creator if you have not created a cover offline.

When you click to create a cover, the sequence will be as follows

Launching Cover Creator...

You will then see

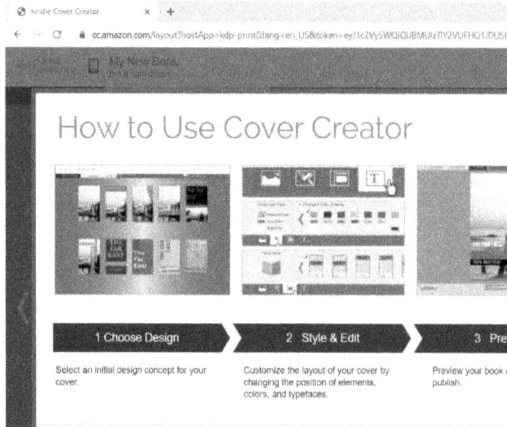

Then you will see the image above. Click on continue. Then, pick a front cover image from your computer that you have previously created. From the panel below, pick the middle option *From My Computer* below. Load file name as previously stored

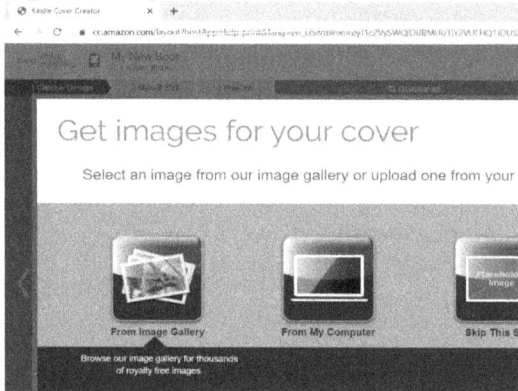

You will see a panel with your image on six designs:

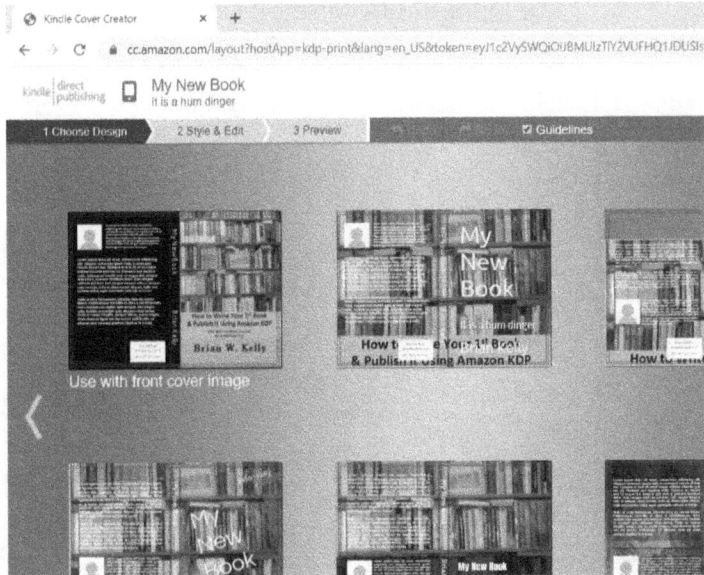

Click on the top left image.

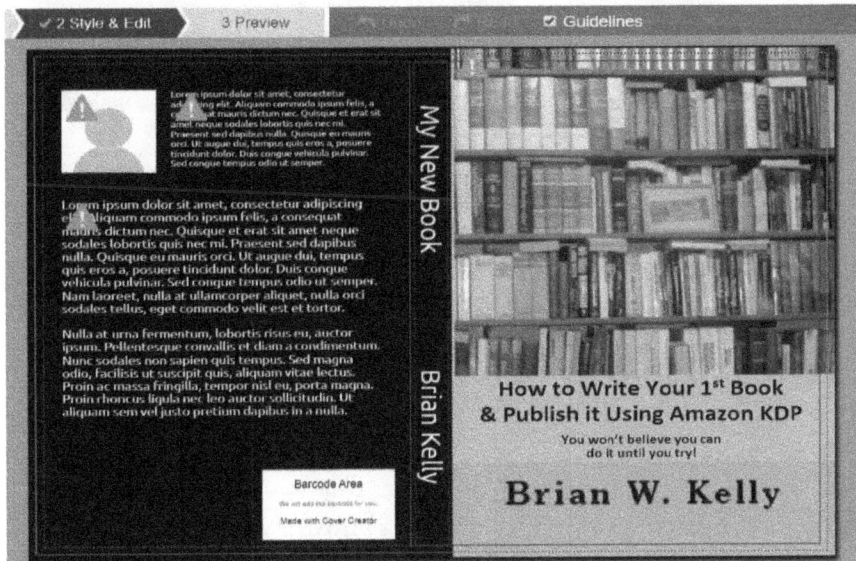

Your front cover appears on the right . On the bottom left is an area in which you can paste the back cover descriptive text for your book. On the upper left, you can copy about your author text. When you click on the image, you can direct the system to find a picture of yourself to use as the author. When you do all that, your cover work screen will look like the image below:

Figure 9-8 Completed Cover

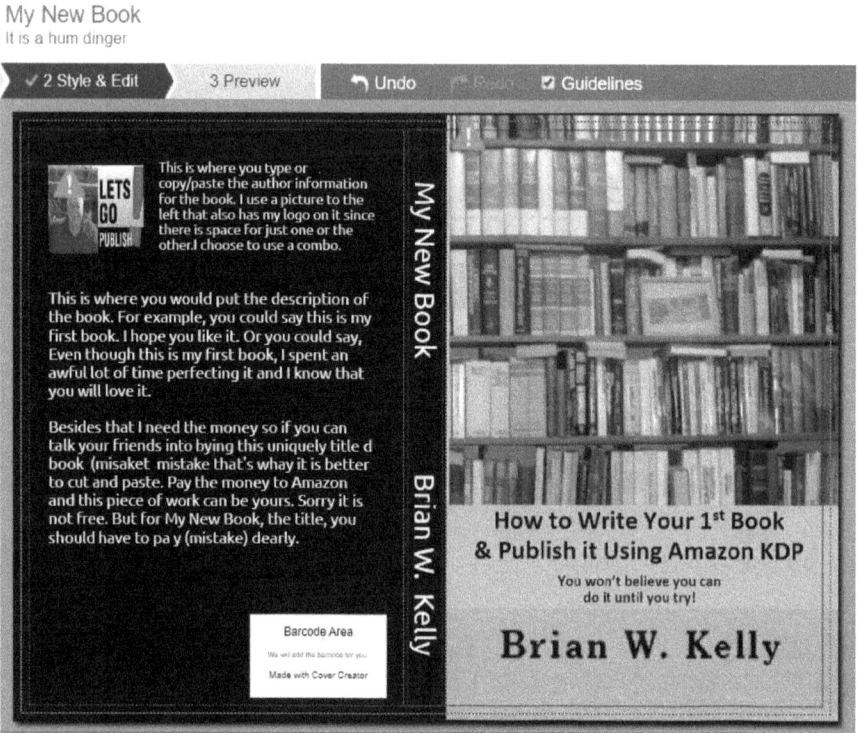

At this point your manuscript file has been uploaded to CreateSpace and it has passed most of the edit checks. Unless there is a big error message (coming up) we may choose to ignore it or proceed with the file as is. If we do not like what we see, we go back to Word, or Cover Creator and make the necessary changes, create a new pdf and upload it until we are OK with what the Auto-Reviewer shows us. That process is coming up after we OK the cover.

With Figure 9-9 showing there are also two buttons on the bottom of this page – Save and Preview

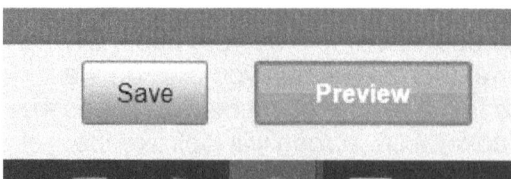

Click on Save and when the machine comes back, click on preview. The machine will create your cover and ask you to submit it

Click on Save & Submit to continue the process

One last step to publish:

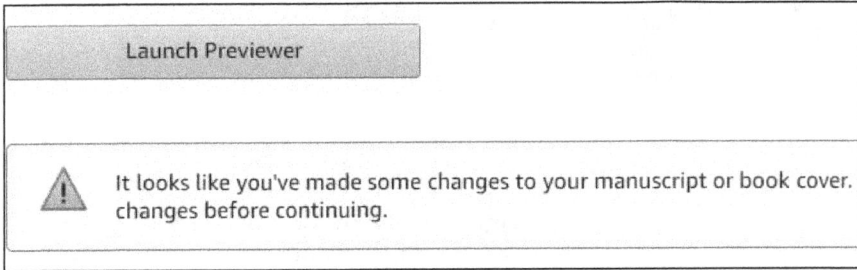

The book is almost finished. When you click on Launch Previewer, you are telling the machine to assemble the whole book and check everything about it and then to give you a preview of every page in the book for your review. If there is an error or you don't like something, your remedy is to go back to the word doc and make your changes. If it's a cover issue, change your offline cover image or your pdf professional cover, if need be and upload them again. Eventually you will come back to get another launch preview until you are satisfied.

When the system thinks you are finished, it gives one last look at the cover and an opportunity to page through the book

After you click on Page advance once, you can look at each page in twos to see if things look as you expect. Odd Page #1 of the front matter is shown on the next page of this book.

To page through your file and see the issue identified in the upload / preparation process, click on the page advance button >

To end the interior review session, either click on exit or after you checked it all out, click on the Approve button at the bottom right

After clicking APPROVE, you will go back to the detail work area where the machine will ask a few more questions such as where you want to sell the book and what the price will be for this book.

Click on **Publish Your Paperback Book** to finish the process. After this, your book is approved and about a day or so later, it is for sale and appears on your bookshelf viewable when you sign on the next time.

LETS GO PUBLISH! Books by Brian Kelly: (Sold at www.bookhawkers.com; Amazon.com, and Kindle.).

Other Books by Brian Kelly: (amazon.com, and Kindle)

How the Philadelphia Eagles Lost Its Karma. This is the one place that tells the story
Cancel All Student Debt Now! Good for America, Good for the Economy.
Social Security Screw Job!!! Scandal: Seniors Intentionally Screwed by US Government
Trump Hate They hate Trump Supporters; Trump; & God—in that order
Christmas Wings for Brian A heartwarming story of a boy whose shoulders kept growing
Merry Christmas to Wilkes-Barre 50 Ways" for Mayor George Brown to Create a Better City.
Air Force Football Championship Seasons From AF Championship to Coach Calhoun's latest team
Syracuse Football Championship Seasons beginning of SU championships; goes to Dino Babers Era
Navy Football Championship Seasons 1st Navy Championships to the Ken Niumatalolo Era
Army Football Championship Seasons Beginning of Football championships to Jeff Monken Era
Florida Gators Championship Seasons Beginning of Football to championships to Dan Mullen era
Alabama's Championship Seasons Beginning of Football past the 2017/2018 National Championship
Clemson Tigers Championship Seasons Beginning of Football to the Clemson Nat Championships
Penn State's Championship Seasons PSU's first championship to the James Franklin era
Notre Dame's Championship Seasons Before Knute Rockne&past Lou Holtz's 1988 undisputed title
Super Bowls & Championship Seasons: The New York Giants Many championships of the Giants.
Super Bowls & Championship Seasons: New England Patriots Many championships of the Patriots.
Super Bowls & Championship Seasons: The Pittsburgh Steelers Many championship of the Steelers.
Super Bowls & Championship Seasons: The Philadelphia Eagles Many championships of the Eagles.
The Big Toxic School Wilkes-Barre Area's Tale of Corruption, Deception, Taxation & Tyranny
Great Players in New York Giants Football Begins with great players of 1925 to Saquon Barqley era.
Great Coaches in New York Giants Football Begins with Bob Folwell 1925 to Pat Shurmur in 2019.
Great Moments in New York Giants Football Beginning of Football to the Pat Shurmur era.
Hasta La Vista California Give California its independence.
IT's ALL OVER! Mueller: "NO COLLUSION!"—Top Dems going to jail for the hoax!
Democrat Secret for Power & Winning Elections Open borders adds millions of new Democrat Voters
Hope for Wilkes-Barre—John Q. Doe—Next Mayor of Wilkes-Barre
The John Doe Plan & WB Plan will help create a better city!
Great Moments in New England Patriots Football Second Edition
This book begins at the beginning of Football and goes to the Bill Belichick era.
The Cowardly Congress Corrupt US Congress is against America and Americans.
Great Players in Air Force Football From the beginning to the current season
Great Coaches in Air Force Football Grom the beginning to Coach Troy Calhoun
Help for Mayor George and Next Mayor of Wilkes-Barre How to vote for the next Mayor Council
Ghost of Wilkes-Barre Future: Spirit's advice for residents how to pick the next Mayor and Council
Great Players in Air Force Football: Air Force's best players of all time
Great Coaches in Air Force Football: From Coach 1 to Coach Troy Calhoun
Great Moments in Air Force Football: From day 1 to today
Great Players in Navy Football: Navy's best including Bellino & Staubach
Great Coaches in Navy Football: From Coach 1 to Coach #39 Ken Niumatalolo
Great Moments in Navy Football: From day 1 to coach Ken Niumatalolo l
No Tree! No Toys! No Toot! Heartwarming story. Christmas gone while 19 month old napped
How to End DACA, Sanctuary Cities, & Resident Illegal Aliens . best solution to remove shadows
Government Must Stop Ripping Off Seniors' Social Security!: Hey buddy, seniors can't spare a dime?
Special Report: Solving America's Student Debt Crisis!: The real solution to the $1.52 Trillion debt
The Winning Political Platform for America Unique winning approach solve big problems in America.
Lou Barletta v Bob Casey for US Senate Barletta's unique approach to solve big problems in America.
John Chrin v Matt Cartwright for Congress Chrin has a unique approach solve big problems in America.
The Cure for Hate !!! Can the cure be any worse than this disease that is crippling America?
Andrew Cuomo's Time to Go? "He Was Never that Great!"**:** Cuomo says America never that great
White People Are Bad! Bad! Bad! Whoever thought a popular slogan in 2018 *It's OK to be White!*
The Fake News Media Is Also Corrupt !!!: Fake press / media today not worthy to be 4th Estate.
God Gave US Donald Trump? Trump was sent from God as the people's answer

Millennials Say America Was "Never That Great": Too many pleased days of political chumps not over!
It's Time for The John Q. Doe Party… Don't you think? By Elephants.
Great Players in Florida Gators Football… Tim Tebow and a ton of other great players
Great Coaches in Florida Gators Football… The best coaches in Gator history.
The Constitution by Hamilton, Jefferson, Madison, et al. The Real Constitution
The Constitution Companion. Will help you learn and understand the Constitution
Great Coaches in Clemson Football The best Clemson Coaches right to Dabo Swinney
Great Players in Clemson Football The best Clemson players in history
Winning Back America. America's been stolen and can be won back completely
The Founding of America… Great book to pick up a lot of great facts
Defeating America's Career Politicians. The scoundrels need to go.
Midnight Mass by Jack Lammers… You remember what it was like Great story
The Bike by Jack Lammers… Great heartwarming Story by Jack
Wipe Out All Student Loan Debt--Now! Watch the economy go boom!
No Free Lunch Pay Back Welfare! Why not pay it back?
Deport All Millennials Now!!! Why they deserve to be deported and/or saved
DELETE the EPA, Please! The worst decisions to hurt America
Taxation Without Representation 4th Edition Should we throw the TEA overboard again?
Four Great Political Essays by Thomas Dawson
Top Ten Political Books for 2018… Cliffnotes Version of 10 Political Books
Top Six Patriotic Books for 2018… Cliffnotes version of 6 Patriotic Boosk
Why Trump Got Elected!.. It's great to hear about a great milestone in America!
The Day the Free Press Died. Corrupt Press Lives on!
Solved (Immigration) The best solutions for 2018
Solved II (Obamacare, Social Security, Student Debt) Check it out; They're solved.
Great Moments in Pittsburgh Steelers Football... Six Super Bowls and more.
Great Players in Pittsburgh Steelers Football ,,,Chuck Noll, Bill Cowher, Mike Tomin, etc.
Great Coaches in New England Patriots Football,,, Bill Belichick the one and only plus others
Great Players in New England Patriots Football… Tom Brady, Drew Bledsoe et al.
Great Coaches in Philadelphia Eagles Football..Andy Reid, Doug Pederson & Lots more
Great Players in Philadelphia Eagles Football Great players such as Sonny Jurgenson
Great Coaches in Syracuse Football All the greats including Ben Schwartzwalder
Great Players in Syracuse Football. Highlights best players such as Jim Brown & Donovan McNabb
Millennials are People Too !!! Give US millennials help to live American Dream
Brian Kelly for the United States Senate from PA: Fresh Face for US Senate
The Candidate's Bible. Don't pray for your campaign without this bible
Rush Limbaugh's Platform for Americans… Rush will love it
Sean Hannity's Platform for Americans… Sean will love it
Donald Trump's New Platform for Americans. Make Trump unbeatable in 2020
Tariffs Are Good for America! One of the best tools a president can have
Great Coaches in Pittsburgh Steelers Football Sixteen of the best coaches ever to coach in pro football.
Great Moments in New England Patriots Football Great football moments from Boston to New England
Great Moments in Philadelphia Eagles Football. The best from the Eagles from the beginning of football.
Great Moments in Syracuse Football The great moments, coaches & players in Syracuse Football
Boost Social Security Now! Hey Buddy Can You Spare a Dime?
The Birth of American Football. From the first college game in 1869 to the last Super Bowl
Obamacare: A One-Line Repeal Congress must get this done.
A Wilkes-Barre Christmas Story A wonderful town makes Christmas all the better
A Boy, A Bike, A Train, and a Christmas Miracle A Christmas story that will melt your heart
Pay-to-Go   America-First Immigration Fix
Legalizing Illegal Aliens Via Resident Visas Americans-first plan saves $Trillions. Learn how!
60 Million Illegal Aliens in America!!! A simple, America-first solution.
The Bill of Rights By Founder James Madison Refresh *your knowledge of the specific rights for all*
Great Players in Army Football Great Army Football played by great players..
Great Coaches in Army Football Army's coaches are all great.
Great Moments in Army Football Army Football at its best.
Great Moments in Florida Gators Football Gators Football from the start. This is the book.
Great Moments in Clemson Football CU Football at its best. This is the book.
Great Moments in Florida Gators Football Gators Football from the start. This is the book.
The Constitution Companion. A Guide to Reading and Comprehending the Constitution
The Constitution by Hamilton, Jefferson, & Madison – Big type and in English
PATERNO: The Dark Days After Win # 409. Sky began to fall within days of win # 409.
JoePa 409 Victories: Say No More! Winningest Division I-A football coach ever
American College Football: The Beginning From before day one football was played.
Great Coaches in Alabama Football Challenging the coaches of every other program!
Great Coaches in Penn State Football the Best Coaches in PSU's football program

Great Players in Penn State Football The best players in PSU's football program
Great Players in Notre Dame Football The best players in ND's football program
Great Coaches in Notre Dame Football The best coaches in any football program
Great Players in Alabama Football from Quarterbacks to offensive Linemen Greats!
Great Moments in Alabama Football AU Football from the start. This is the book.
Great Moments in Penn State Football PSU Football, start--games, coaches, players,
Great Moments in Notre Dame Football ND Football, start, games, coaches, players
Cross Country with the Parents A great trip from East Coast to West with the kids
Seniors, Social Security & the Minimum Wage. Things seniors need to know.
How to Write Your First Book and Publish It with CreateSpace. You too can be an author.
The US Immigration Fix--It's all in here. Finally, an answer.
I had a Dream IBM Could be #1 Again The title is self-explanatory
WineDiets.Com Presents The Wine Diet Learn how to lose weight while having fun.
Wilkes-Barre, PA; Return to Glory Wilkes-Barre City's return to glory
Geoffrey Parsons' Epoch... The Land of Fair Play Better than the original.
The Bill of Rights 4 Dummmies! This is the best book to learn about your rights.
Sol Bloom's Epoch ...Story of the Constitution The best book to learn the Constitution
America 4 Dummmies! All Americans should read to learn about this great country.
The Electoral College 4 Dummmies! How does it really work?
The All-Everything Machine Story about IBM's finest computer server.
ThankYou IBM! This book explains how IBM was beaten in the computer marketplace by neophytes

Amazon.com/author/brianwkelly
Brian W. Kelly has written 232 books including this one.
Thank you for buying this book and the others.
Others can be found at amazon.com/author/brianwkelly
I would be thrilled if you bought a book from me, Brian Kelly.

www.ingramcontent.com/pod-product-compliance
Lightning Source LLC
LaVergne TN
LVHW041159080426
835511LV00006B/668